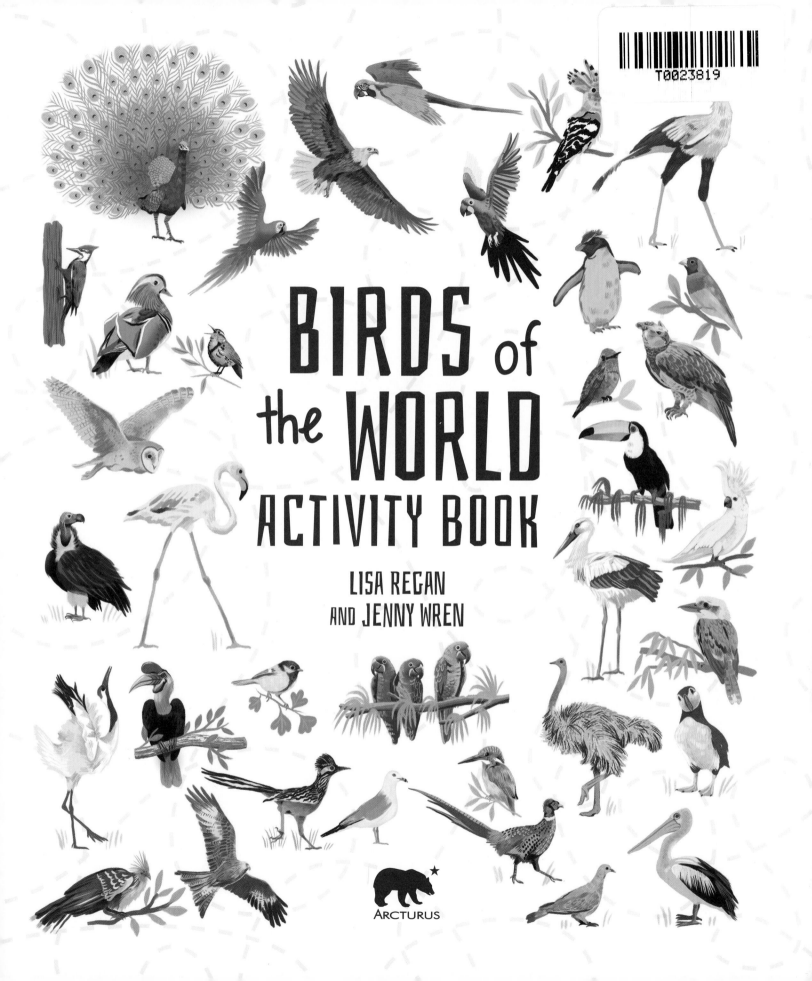

BIRDS of the WORLD
ACTIVITY BOOK

LISA REGAN
AND JENNY WREN

ARCTURUS

ARCTURUS

This edition published in 2024 by Arcturus Publishing Limited
26/27 Bickels Yard, 151–153 Bermondsey Street,
London SE1 3HA

Author: Lisa Regan
Illustrator: Jenny Wren
Consultant: Anne Rooney
Editor: Violet Peto
Designer: Rosie Bellwood-Moyler
Design Manager: Jessica Holliland
Managing Editor: Joe Harris

ISBN: 978-1-3988-3681-5
CH010503NT
Supplier 29, Date 1123, PI 00004296

Printed in China

CONTENTS

WHAT MAKES A BIRD?   4

IN THE AIR   6

BREEDING AND NESTING   8

LIFESTYLES   10

NORTH AMERICA   12

SOUTH AMERICA   22

EUROPE   38

ANTARCTICA   52

AFRICA   56

ASIA   68

OCEANIA   76

ANSWERS   88

WHAT MAKES A BIRD?

Birds are warm-blooded vertebrates (which is to say, animals with a backbone) that breathe air. They are the only living creatures with feathers. They have several other distinctive features, including wings and a beak or bill. Birds reproduce by laying eggs.

FEATHER FUNCTIONS

A bird's feathers help it to conserve body heat, and also to stay dry. Down feathers sit next to the skin and are short and fluffy for insulation. Contour feathers are smooth with a central shaft. They are naturally water-repellent. Flight feathers on the wings and tail help to create lift, so the birds can move through the air.

Match each of these feathers to the bird it came from.

A

B

C

D

E

1

2

3

4

5

BILLS

The shape of the bill is usually an indication of what the bird eats, often tailored to a special kind of diet such as fish, seeds, fruit, or meat.

- Some bills are so distinctive, you can tell immediately what the bird is.

Can you match each of these pictures to the correct bird name?

Flamingo

Toucan

Puffin

Hummingbird

Pelican

ON THE INSIDE

A bird has fewer bones than a mammal. Birds that can fly generally have hollow bones, to make them lighter. They also have a large ridge on their breastbone, called a keel. Powerful flight muscles attach to this keel, giving birds the strength to take off and fly.

- Powerful fliers, such as pigeons and doves, have a higher than usual percentage of flight muscles.

Do the mathematics here, then cross out any answer that gives an odd number. The remaining number is the percentage of a bird's body weight that is made up by flight muscles.

90÷2

3 x 25

17 + 32

79 – 42

81÷3

17 x 3

8 x 5

105÷7

IN THE AIR

A bird's wings have bones inside. The wings are similar to a human arm, with joints like the wrist, shoulder, and elbow that enables the wing to open, close, and swivel. The feathers create lift, carrying a bird up, up, and away. Generally, a bird uses its wings to adjust its height and flying speed, and steers with its tail.

WINGS

A bird's wingspan is the distance across both wings, measured from tip to tip. Wingspan and wing shape varies greatly. Birds that glide have long, stiff, narrow wings. Birds that fly quickly, such as the swift, have curved wings that point backward.

1. Largest wingspan
2. Smallest wingspan
3. Highest flying bird
4. Fastest beating wings
5. Longest time in the air
6. Heaviest flying bird
7. Longest migration

▪ Flying lets a bird escape predators, find and catch food, meet a mate, and travel huge distances to avoid cold, harsh winters.

Use the code key to work out which bird holds each of these records.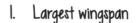

A	🕯	N	◆
B	✏	O	●
C	⏳	P	✿
D	👌	Q	⌘
E	👍	R	❀
F	☺	S	◎
G	☼	T	✳
H	💧	U	❄
I	❄	V	◇
J	☠	W	★
K	💣	X	○
L	✈	Y	■
M	▢	Z	◣
	-		📫

1 ★🕯◆👌👍✿✳◆☼ 🕯✈✏🕯✳✿●◎◎

2 ✏👍👍 💧✳▢▢✳◆☼✏✳✿👌

3 ☼❀✳☺☺●◆ ◇✳✈✳✳❀👍

4 ✿✳✏■▢📫✳💧❀●🕯✳👍👌 💧✳▢▢✳◆☼✏✳❀👌

5 ⏳●▢▢●◆ ◎★✳☺✳

6 ✏✳◎✳🕯✿👌

7 🕯✿⏳✳❄✳⏳ ✳👍✿◆

6

FLIGHTLESS BIRDS

Some birds have abandoned flight altogether. Ratites are mostly large birds with long legs, such as the ostrich and emu, which have become fast runners instead. Penguins use their wings like flippers, to propel them through the water at top speed.

Follow the trails to find out where each of these flightless birds makes its home. Find out more about each of them later in the book.

Kiwi

Rhea

Cassowary

Emu

Emperor penguin

Ostrich

South America

Africa

Antarctica

New Zealand

Australia

New Guinea and Australia

▪ An ostrich has large wings but it uses them to help steer and balance when it runs instead of using them to fly. They also spread their wings to show off, and to provide shade from the hot sun.

7

BREEDING AND NESTING

When it comes to breeding, timing is often vital. Near the equator, birds may breed all year round. However in temperate regions, the breeding time is determined by the seasons, temperature, and length of the day. Once they have found a mate, birds build a nest, lay their eggs, and wait for their chicks to hatch.

GETTING TOGETHER

Many birds are monogamous: They find a breeding partner and stay together all year, sometimes for their whole life. Others, such as the bowerbird, are polygamous: The male mates with as many partners as he can.

Some birds are famous for their courtship rituals. They may dance and strut to attract a mate. Songbirds use their vocal talents to show off. Others, like peacocks, have elaborate plumage to show how strong and healthy they are. Finish the picture of this peacock to help him show off his amazing tail.

NESTING

A nest is a safe place to lay eggs and bring up chicks. This may be inside a tree, or in a hole in a cliff. Some are huge or elaborate shapes. Others are simple scrapes in the ground.

This bird lays its eggs on the beach, so its eggs are disguised to look like pebbles. Work out what the bird is called by moving each letter one letter back in the alphabet.

SJOHFE QMPWFS

BABY BIRDS

A newborn chick (a hatchling) will most likely be a scrawny, featherless little thing that cannot look after itself. After a few days, it will be covered in fluffy down. A fledgling has more feathers and is getting ready to leave the nest and attempt to fly.

- Some baby birds are precocial: they are born with their eyes open, with fluffy down feathers, and are able to leave the nest very early on. Chickens, geese, and ducks are all examples.

- A baby bird has a special bump on its beak, called an egg tooth. It uses it to break its way out from inside the egg. The egg tooth disappears as the chick gets older.

See if you can spot six differences between these two pictures of a mother duck and her young ducklings.

PARENTAL CARE

Before an egg hatches, its parents must keep it warm. This is known as incubation, and is done by either parent, depending on the species. After hatching, the chicks need food, and lots of it.

Certain species, especially flamingos, pelicans, and ostriches, leave their chicks in a nursery. The large group is cared for by one or a few adults.

START

Help this ostrich chick find its way back to the others.

FINISH

LIFESTYLES

Like other living creatures, birds have adapted their lifestyles to suit their surroundings. They may deal with changing seasons by migrating or sleeping. They feed at different times of day, in a variety of locations, and on a wide range of foods.

MIGRATION

The ability to fly makes birds some of the most mobile creatures on the planet. Over half of the world's birds split their time between locations. They may travel long distances to find food all year round, and to raise their young in the best surroundings.

Use every third letter to spell the name for any type of bird that doesn't migrate but stays in the same region all year round.

HIBERNATION

When winter comes, not all birds fly to warmer places. Some go into a kind of semi-hibernation known as torpor. Their body temperature drops and they remain inactive.

Find each of the birds from the list in this grid. The words can appear up and down, across, or diagonally, and forward or backward.

T	B	F	R	O	G	L	M	D	C
A	H	D	O	R	M	L	R	S	H
D	L	G	M	O	S	I	C	C	I
R	L	D	I	A	B	W	H	O	C
O	I	G	R	N	D	T	I	U	K
A	W	E	U	M	R	I	C	F	S
D	R	S	N	O	I	C	K	T	T
R	O	R	N	U	B	H	A	I	M
U	O	V	E	T	G	I	D	N	O
N	S	D	E	H	N	V	E	G	V
N	P	F	S	W	I	S	E	F	E
E	C	R	U	N	M	O	D	O	E
R	F	R	O	G	M	O	U	T	H
S	W	G	C	S	U	R	S	R	C
L	R	N	O	G	H	T	I	A	H
S	N	I	G	H	T	H	A	W	K

Hummingbird

Dove

Nighthawk

Sunbird

Frogmouth

Roadrunner

Swift

Chickadee

ON THE MENU

Different birds have different diets. Some have a plant-based diet, ranging from nectar and pollen to fruit and seeds. Even more rely on animal-based foods, including eggs, carrion (dead animals), insects, fish, and other water creatures such as larvae and crustaceans.

See which puzzle piece is not needed to finish this picture of some feeding North American birds.

- Owls and other raptors (see page 46) hunt by catching live prey in their talons. They are known collectively as birds of prey.

A

B

C

D

E

F

G

NORTH AMERICA

This continent stretches from the icy Arctic Circle in the north to the Caribbean Islands, almost on the equator. It has mountains, deserts, grassland, and tundra, so the variety of birdlife is astonishing and wonderful.

HUMMINGBIRD

Hummingbirds are only found in the Americas. They can hover, fly backward, and even fly upside down. It helps them to feed on the nectar of flowers.

- The most common one in the US is the ruby-throated hummingbird seen here.

Ih
N a
Sr
pr
b
E
Cf
T
Sa
id

Cross out the letters in lower case. Use the remaining letters to spell another item on a hummingbird's menu.

- -

- Their name comes from the humming sound made by their wings beating so quickly.

- The smallest bird in the world is Cuba's bee hummingbird. Its wingspan is the length of a paperclip.

CANADA GOOSE

These birds are a common sight in North America. They are famous for flying south in the winter to avoid the harshest weather.

Which one of these flying geese does not have a matching silhouette below?

- Canada geese form a V-shape when they fly in flocks. This pattern helps them keep track of each other.

A B C D E F G

- Canada geese take turns at the front of the V-shape. This lets the others save their energy, because the bird at the front deals with the most air resistance.

MEADOWLARK

Noted for its song, this bird is the state bird of six states.

Can you find the names of all six states in this word spiral? Cross out any U, C, F, or V that you find.

- The Western meadowlark is about the size of a robin but with a short tail. The males can be seen and heard perched on top of fence posts, bushes, and power lines.

BALD EAGLE

This distinctive bird is an emblem of the United States.

Figure out the numbers in this pyramid puzzle to find out what year it officially became the country's national symbol. The value of a square is the sum of the two numbers directly beneath it.

| 8 |
| 6 | 3 | 69 |

- Bald eagles build their nests at the top of very tall trees, to keep them safe. Many of them return to the same nest each year, making it bigger and better.

- They line the nest with soft moss, and lay one to three eggs inside.

- Bald eagles eat fish, spotting them from high up and swooping down to grab them with their feet.

PELICAN

Here's another bird that feasts on fish! Count how many flapping fish are in this pool for the pelican to scoop up.

- The white pelican is one of North America's largest birds. Its wingspan is about 2.75 m (9 ft) across.

- During the breeding season, pelicans grow an extra "horn" on top of their beak.

- These birds are famous for the pouch beneath their bill, which can stretch to hold large amounts of fish.

CHICKADEE

There are several types of chickadees living in North America. Their name comes from the noise they make.

These birds store excess food to eat later. This storage place has a special name. Use the code to work out what it is.

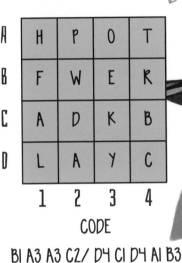

	1	2	3	4
A	H	P	O	T
B	F	W	E	R
C	A	D	K	B
D	L	A	Y	C

CODE

B1 A3 A3 C2/ D4 C1 D4 A1 B3

CHESTNUT-BACKED CHICKADEE

BLACK-CAPPED CHICKADEE

- To attract these birds to your yard, put out the foods they like: mealworms, peanut pieces, sunflower seeds, raisins, and nut pieces.

- Many black-capped chickadees will happily eat seeds out of your hand.

BLUE JAY

Here's another bird that can be attracted to your home by putting out seeds. Its gorgeous blue feathers and distinctive head crest make it easy to spot.

- They love to eat acorns, and help to spread them by burying them far and wide, and forgetting about them.

Copy the plumage of this blue jay onto the black and white version.

GULL

Often known as a seagull, this bird's proper name is the ring-billed gull. Bizarrely, it is seen as often inland as at the coast.

These large birds have a reputation for stealing food, often from other birds, but also from people! Match each one to the snack it has stolen.

CROW

The American crow is a noisy bird that makes a hoarse cawing sound. They are very intelligent birds that can use tools. Crows will eat almost anything, including fruit, nuts, insects, frogs, and small mammals.

Help the crow find a way out of the maze collecting every item of food.

PEREGRINE FALCON

A truly majestic bird of prey, the peregrine falcon is found on six continents, but is still quite a rare sight.

Study the facts, then turn the book upside down and answer the questions below.

▪ By the 1970s it was seriously endangered because of the effects of pesticides in its diet. Thankfully, its numbers have risen again through breeding projects in captivity.

▪ They are the world's fastest bird, diving through the air at speeds around 320 km/h (200 mph.)

▪ Some peregrine falcons live up to 17 years in the wild.

▪ If their cliff nesting sites aren't available, they will sometimes live in the city on pylons, bridges, and skyscrapers.

▪ They hunt in midair, dropping down on their prey from above. This dive is called a stoop.

▪ They feed mostly on birds but occasionally eat bats and other small mammals, lizards, frogs, and insects.

5. What caused them to become endangered?

4. Outside the city, where do they commonly lay their eggs?

3. How fast is their dive?

2. What kind of flying mammal might they eat?

1. What name is given to their top speed dive?

AMERICAN GOLDFINCH

Listen for the call of these small birds as they fly; many people say it sounds like "po-ta-to-chip" or "perchickory."

These birds are yellow only if they are male, and even then only at certain times of the year. Use the code on the tree to find out when this is.

9.14 / 20.8.5 / 19.16.18.9.14.7 / 1.14.4 / 19.21.13.13.5.18

WOODPECKER

This bird pecks at trees to feed on carpenter ants and their larvae, leaving large rectangular holes in the trunk.

Their distinctive drumming noise isn't only the sound of drilling for food. They also use it to attract a mate or warn others off their territory.

Use the code on the tree to figure out the name of this woodpecker. It is the largest one found in North America.

16.9.12.5.1.20.5.4 / 23.15.15.4.16.5.3.11.5.18

A=1
B=2
C=3
D=4
E=5
F=6
G=7
H=8
I=9
J=10
K=11
L=12
M=13
N=14
O=15
P=16
Q=17
R=18
S=19
T=20
U=21
V=22
W=23
X=24
Y=25
Z=26

LOON

The beautiful black and white feathers of the common loon make it a marvel to look at. This bird's haunting calls can be heard across lakes in Canada and much of the US. They are strong swimmers and powerful divers, but clumsy if they have to walk on land.

These loon parents have got lots of babies between them. How many can you spot?

▪ Their bold summer patterns fade for the winter.

BURROWING OWL

These intriguing birds have a brown and white speckled body and long legs. They hunt during both day and night. Most notably, they live in social groups in underground tunnels.

▪ Depending on where they live, some owls dig their own burrows, while others move into old burrows left by prairie dogs, armadillos, or other animals.

Figure out in which order they need to visit each of these tunnels.

1. First, they dip into their collection of bottle caps to decorate the entrance.

2. Then they drop off more centipedes in the food store.

3. Next, they check on their eggs.

4. Finally, they snack on a scorpion.

ROADRUNNER

A type of cuckoo that is found in Mexico and the southern US, the greater roadrunner CAN fly, but it much prefers to run.

Which of these racing roadrunners doesn't have an exact match?

- It has strong legs and can reach speeds up to 30 km/h (18 mph) over short sprints.

- As desert dwellers, they barely need to drink, but get plenty of moisture from their food.

TURKEY

Another American icon, the wild turkey lives throughout much of the US and Mexico. The males are large, heavy birds with a fan-shaped tail. They live in woodland and forests, mostly foraging on the ground for roots, seeds, and berries.

Follow the steps and draw your own wild turkey here.

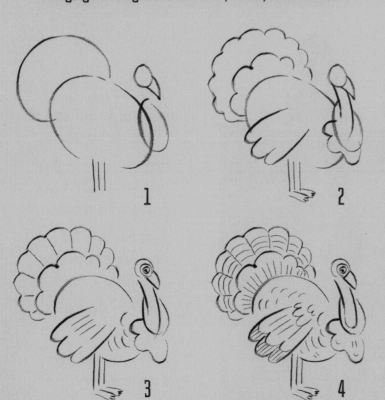

MALLARD DUCK

Mallards are the most commonly seen duck, not only in North America but across the whole northern hemisphere. You've probably seen them on a pond, lake, or river. When feeding, they "dabble" with their head down and feet and tail up in the air.

- Male ducks are called drakes and have a distinctive green head and yellow bill. They also have a rich chestnut-brown breast and a white ring around their neck.

- Ducklings can swim when they are only a day or two old.

These ducklings are trying to keep up with their parents. Which one doesn't appear in the second picture?

ROBIN

With its orange-red chest and bright yellow beak, this bird is easy to spot and identify. This is an American robin, and is bigger and slimmer than the European robin. It is a social bird that gathers in flocks, while the European robin is solitary and territorial.

Which puzzle pieces are not needed to complete the picture?

- They love to eat earthworms, especially first thing in the morning, and berries.

- They lay bright blue eggs. When the chicks hatch, both parents bring them food.

A

B

C

D

E

SOUTH AMERICA

This continent lies mostly in the southern hemisphere, and reaches all the way from the equator almost to the Antarctic Circle. It is home to the Amazon rain forest, with an astonishing variety of birds. South America's bird life ranges from penguins to parrots, and scarlet macaws to blue-footed boobies.

HOATZIN

This bird has a head that seems too small for its body, red eyes, a spiky mohawk, and a blue featherless face. It shuffles clumsily on the ground or in low branches, making loud huffing noises.

Decide whether these statements about the hoatzin are true or false. If you're not sure, use the number clues to help you.

1. The adult birds smell like fresh cow dung.

2. They enjoy sunbathing and often perch with their wings spread in the sun.

3. They mostly eat dead things, from rotting vegetation to animal carcasses.

4. To avoid predators, the chicks plop into the water and hide under the surface.

5. They are skilled fliers and can navigate through the Amazon rain forest with ease.

6. Adults are about the size of a blackbird.

Clues:
Two out of the three true facts are even numbers.
Two out of the three false statements are prime numbers.
The first fact is true.

JACAMAR

There are around 18 species of jacamar living in South and Central America. They are fairly small birds with a long bill and often have glossy feathers in iridescent jewel shades.

- They mostly eat flying insects, catching wasps, dragonflies, and butterflies in midair.

A	B	D	E	G	H	I	L	N	P	R	S
★	✸	◎	⏶	◆	✿	⌘	■	☯	●	❄	⬥

They are often named for their appearance, such as the green-tailed jacamar, white-eared jacamar, and yellow-billed jacamar. This one has a slightly different name; use the code to work out what it is called.

● ★ ❄ ★ ◎ ⌘ ⬥ ⏶

RHEA

There are two types of rhea, both flightless, and both native to South America. They live in grasslands and dry areas.

Work your way up and down the list of zoologists and naturalists to discover who the lesser rhea is named after.

1. Lamarck
2. Linnaeus
3. Durrell
4. Goodall
5. Darwin
6. Flannery
7. Fossey
8. Humboldt
9. Suzuki
10. Attenborough
11. Cuvier
12. Rothschild

Begin at the bottom. Climb 8 names to a woman who studied chimpanzees. Drop 4 names to a man with penguins and many species named after him. Drop 2 more to a British broadcaster and environmentalist. Climb 8 to the man who shaped the way we describe the animal and plant kingdoms. Move 3 places lower to find the man you're looking for.

- They are fast runners, and run in zigzags to escape from danger.

- They are strong swimmers and can cross large lakes to reach food.

- Like ostriches, the male is in charge of incubating the eggs and caring for the chicks.

- The greater rhea is the largest bird on the continent.

23

QUETZAL

Several species of quetzal are found in South and Central America. Some are famous for their bright green and blue shimmering feathers, or for their trailing tail plumes which can reach up to 90 cm (3 ft) in length.

Which of these silhouettes is an exact match for the resplendent quetzal shown here?

- The long tail plumes are grown by the males during mating season.

- Their iridescent feathers shimmer and shine, giving them camouflage in the forest canopy where they live.

- They feed on all kinds of foods, from fruits to small creatures, such as insects and lizards.

HAWK-HEADED PARROT

This medium-sized parrot lives in the Amazon river basin, usually in the canopy of the rain forest. It can fluff out its long neck feathers to create a fan around its head, making itself look bigger. It is sometimes known as the red fan parrot.

These birds have all got their feathers fluffed! Which one of them is a tiny bit different from the others?

TANAGER

Tanagers are a type of songbird, and there are hundreds of different ones. They are known for their brilliant plumage.

Match these tanagers into pairs, and find one that is on its own.

- Some, such as the scarlet tanager, breed in North America and head to South America for the winter.

HARPY EAGLE

This predator is one of the world's biggest eagles. It lives in South America, mainly in the Amazon rain forest. It can swoop through the trees, snatching prey as it goes.

SLOTH
MONKEY
COATI
SNAKE
PARROT
PORCUPINE
OPOSSUM
ARMADILLO
ANTEATER
KINKAJOU
SQUIRREL
IGUANA

M	A	R	M	S	Q	U	I	R	I	L	L
S	N	P	O	A	N	T	E	A	T	E	R
Q	N	O	P	M	R	A	P	G	K	P	O
U	M	R	K	A	O	N	K	E	I	L	I
I	O	C	I	S	R	I	O	E	N	E	G
A	N	U	N	Q	G	R	P	C	K	R	U
N	K	P	K	U	I	L	O	E	A	R	S
T	E	I	A	R	M	A	S	T	J	I	L
O	Y	N	R	H	T	H	S	P	O	U	O
S	A	E	R	I	T	T	U	A	U	Q	L
N	L	K	I	N	K	O	M	R	P	S	I
A	A	R	M	A	D	I	L	L	O	T	H
P	A	E	A	T	E	R	K	S	R	E	Y

Look for all the listed animals in the grid. Each of them is a likely meal for a hungry harpy eagle. The words can appear up and down and across forward, backward, and diagonally.

MACAW

Macaws are a type of parrot and are often seen flying or perching together in small flocks. The macaw has a long tail, bright feathers, a bare face, and a large, powerful, hooked beak. This beak is strong enough to use as an extra foot, clinging onto branches and hanging upside down.

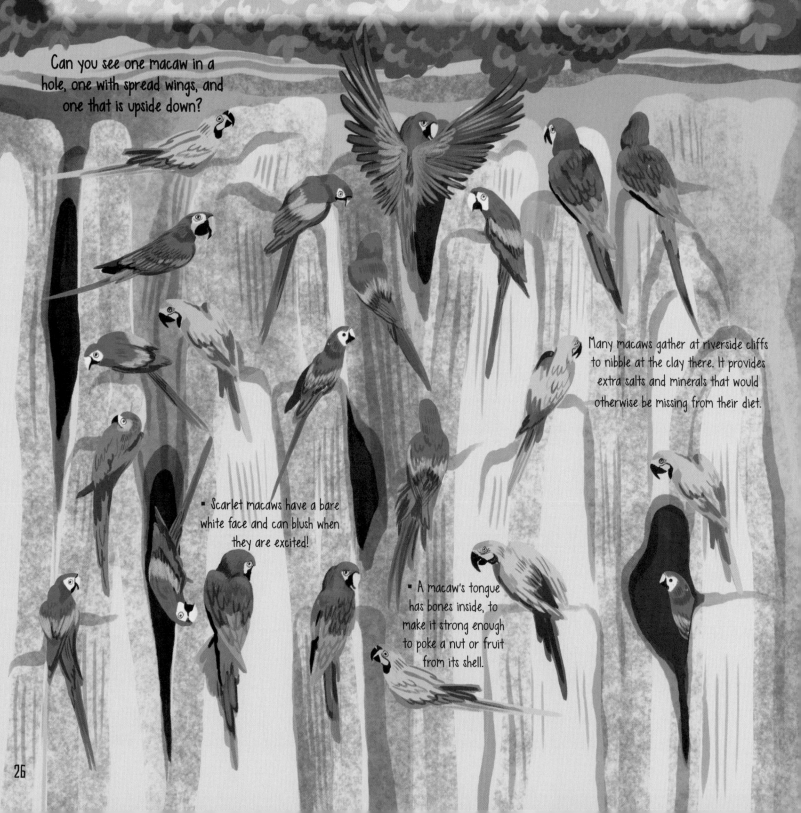

Can you see one macaw in a hole, one with spread wings, and one that is upside down?

Many macaws gather at riverside cliffs to nibble at the clay there. It provides extra salts and minerals that would otherwise be missing from their diet.

▪ Scarlet macaws have a bare white face and can blush when they are excited!

▪ A macaw's tongue has bones inside, to make it strong enough to poke a nut or fruit from its shell.

POTOO

These brown mottled birds are camouflaged to look like tree bark. They spend their day sleeping on dead branches, and awake at dusk to hunt. They are related to nightjars and the frogmouths of Australia.

P	O	T	T	O	T	P	O
O	P	O	P	O	P	O	P
O	T	O	O	O	T	T	O
T	T	P	T	P	T	O	O
O	O	O	O	O	T	O	P
O	O	T	P	O	O	T	O
P	P	O	T	O	O	T	O
P	O	T	O	T	P	O	T

How many times can you find the word POTOO hidden in the grid? It can appear up, down, across, or diagonally, and forward or backward.

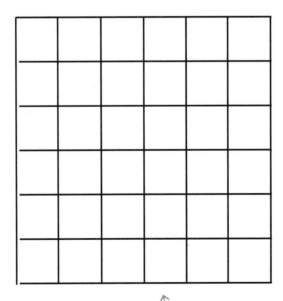

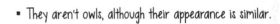

- They aren't owls, although their appearance is similar.

- They have a wide mouth for catching prey as they fly. They eat flying insects.

- They don't build a nest but find a hollow or hole in a branch that will hold their single egg.

Use this grid to help you copy your own beautiful barbet.

BARBET

The scarlet-banded barbet is a medium-sized bird with distinctive plumage. It is found only in a tiny part of Peru, on and around the summit of a single mountain in the Andes. There are thought to be fewer than 1,000 left, and it is classed as being vulnerable to extinction.

TOUCAN

There are several species of toucan, and the toco toucan is the largest of them all. Famous for its huge, orange beak and striking markings, it is an iconic rain forest bird. Which two toucans are an exact match?

- The huge beak is hollow, so it is very light. It is used for reaching fruit on tiny branches that wouldn't support the bird's weight.

- The toucan has a long, flat tongue that is frayed on the edges, making it look like a feather.

- A sleeping toucan turns its head so its bill rests along its back.

COCK OF THE ROCK

This striking bird lives in the cloud forest and eats fruit, and sometimes insects or other creatures. The males have brighter plumage than the females, and jump, dance, and squeal to attract a mate.

Cross out any letter that appears twice. The remaining letters spell the country that has the cock of the rock as its national bird.

RAIN FOREST BIRDS

Around a third of all the world's bird species can be found in the Amazon rain forest. Scientists have classified over 1,300 species, some of which are just passing through or spending the winters there.

See if you can match the descriptions to the correct bird pairs.

- The oropendola is a sleek, dark bird with some yellow tail feathers. It builds an unusual long nest that hangs down from the branches.

- The male scaled antbird is black-and-white speckled.

- The blue-faced capuchinbird is large, with a head that looks too small for its body. Males make a noise that has been described as sounding like a distant chainsaw or cow.

- These birds aren't necessarily all found in the same part of the rain forest. It's an extremely big place!

FRIGATEBIRD

The magnificent frigatebird is a brownish-black seabird that soars above the ocean like a pterodactyl. The females have white chests and the males have bright red sacs on their chest, which they puff out to impress the females.

The bigger the chest, the deeper a male's mating call, which seems to attract more females. Put these male frigatebirds in order of size, from largest to smallest.

- Magnificent frigatebirds eat fish. They don't swim or dive (their feathers aren't waterproof) but swoop low and skim fish, jellyfish, and squid from near the surface.

- Nicknamed pirate birds, they chase other birds in midair and bully them until they drop or regurgitate their recently captured food. Then they dive down and snatch it before it hits the water.

- Young frigatebirds learn this piracy by chasing each other and dropping sticks from their beaks, which other youngsters then catch.

SCREECH OWL

Various species of screech owl are found in South America, including the tawny-bellied and black-capped, but the tropical screech owl is one of the most widespread. It nests in holes in trees and sometimes in termite mounds. It begins hunting at dusk and spends daylight hours roosting in a tree.

Find a pathway through this twilight maze, from start to finish. Which of the prey animals has a lucky escape tonight?

BOOBY

The boobies are a group of seabirds that have big, webbed feet and a strong bill. They grow to at least 0.6 m (2 ft). They generally live over the ocean, and return to shore for breeding. They are agile fliers but clumsy on land. Three of the species can be found on the Galápagos Islands and are famous for their bright feet.

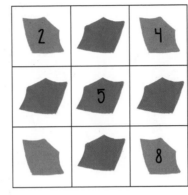

Work out which numbers should go on the blank footprints. Each row, column, and diagonal adds up to 15.

• Blue-footed boobies are comical to watch on dry land. They are well known for their courtship ritual, which involves the male marching around the female, showing off his fabulous blue feet.

• Red-footed boobies have equally vivid feet, but they are of course red. These are the smallest of the booby species.

FINCH

Here's one little bird that makes its presence felt. It's a bloodsucker! It mostly eats seeds, nectar, and insects, but it occasionally drinks the blood of living creatures. It lives on the Galápagos Islands, so boobies are its main prey animals.

YDPSLUH / JURXQG / ILQFK

Use the decoder to figure out the full name of this unusual bird.

D	E	F	G	H	I	J	K	L	M	N	O	P	Q	R	S	T	U	V	W	X	Y	Z	A	B	C
A	B	C	D	E	F	G	H	I	J	K	L	M	N	O	P	Q	R	S	T	U	V	W	X	Y	Z

MANAKIN

There are about 55 species in the manakin family. They are small birds with bright plumage that live in woodland and rain forest.

Can you find each of these?

1. A black bird with a yellow chest.
2. A red bird with black wings.
3. A black bird with a red head.
4. A black bird with blue wings and a red cap.
5. A blue bird with black wings and a red cap.

The males often take part in lekking, a type of courtship ritual:

- The golden-headed manakin hops rapidly between saplings, snapping its wings like firecrackers.

- The wire-tailed manakin moonwalks along a branch and puffs out its feathers.

- The blue manakin leaps and flies in a mesmerizing routine.

ALBATROSS

The waved albatross is an ocean-going marvel. It rarely comes to land, only gathering on South American islands to breed. It is airborne all day and sleeps on the surface of the ocean. It has an extremely energy-efficient method of flying and so can stay in the air for hours without flapping its huge wings.

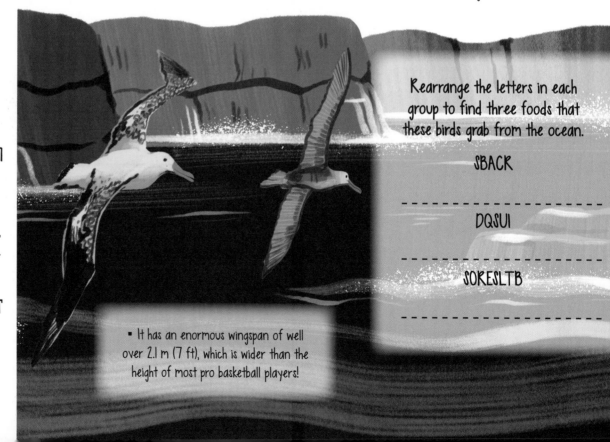

- It has an enormous wingspan of well over 2.1 m (7 ft), which is wider than the height of most pro basketball players!

Rearrange the letters in each group to find three foods that these birds grab from the ocean.

SBACR

DQSUI

SORESLTB

PENGUIN

Several species of penguin can be found in South America. Some gather on remote islands to breed, while others range down long stretches of the west and east coasts. Follow the wiggly lines to find out which live where.

▪ Macaroni penguins have a golden crest and red eyes. They mostly eat krill. A single colony of breeding pairs can contain up to 2.5 million penguins.

1. Peru, Argentina, and Chile

▪ Magellanic penguins make their nests in burrows and under bushes. They hunt at sea in groups, diving down as far as 250 ft (75 m).

3. Chile, Argentina, the Falkland Islands, and Antarctica

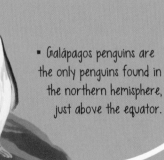

▪ Galápagos penguins are the only penguins found in the northern hemisphere, just above the equator.

2. Patagonia (the southernmost tip of Chile and Argentina) and the Falkland Islands

▪ Humboldt penguins are a type of banded penguin, named for their markings. They make their nests in underground burrows, dug into layers of dried guano (seabird droppings).

4. Galápagos Islands, west of Ecuado

SCARLET IBIS

Living mostly along the coasts of northern South America, these stunning birds gather in huge flocks. They have long, narrow, slightly curved beaks for poking into mud to catch crabs, crayfish, shrimps, snails, frogs, and small fish.

Can you spot seven differences between these two scenes?

- The birds make a loud honking noise to signal danger, to say "hello," and to attract a mate.

INCA TERN

It's hard to ignore the striking ornamental whiskers on this beautiful bird. It has charcoal plumage, a forked tail, plus bright red legs, bill, and webbed feet. Its tuft of white "facial hair" shows how healthy it is; the longer it is, the healthier the bird and the more likely to produce large chicks.

▪ These birds are thieves! They sometimes dive down and snatch fish straight out of the mouth of a sea lion or even a dolphin.

How many fish are there here for the tern to feast on?

CARACARA

The crested caracara is one of the few birds of prey that hunt on foot as well as in the air. They stalk small mammals, reptiles, amphibians, and insects along the ground, and will eat carrion.

START

Help the caracara find a way through the undergrowth to reach the finish.

▪ If they are in danger or excited, the skin on their faces turns yellow instead of red.

FINISH

ANDEAN CONDOR

A type of vulture, this huge bird soars high in the sky over the mountains of South America. It searches for carrion to eat, often covering many miles in a day. It is the largest bird of prey on the planet.

- Their preferred food is the carcasses of large animals, but they do also catch and eat live animals such as rabbits, rodents, and birds.

- They are heavy birds and need air currents to keep them aloft.

Which of the silhouettes is an exact match for the main picture?

JABIRU

This stork is enormous, and so is its bill. It is found in several South American countries but is most common in Brazil and Paraguay's wetlands. It catches live food but also feeds on dead creatures.

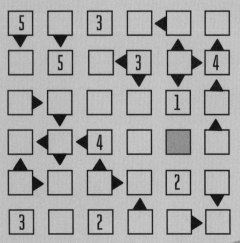

Fill in the missing numbers so that every row and column has the numbers 1 to 6. The arrow always points toward a lower number. The number in the shaded square tells you which of the facts about the jabiru is actually true.

1. It lays the biggest eggs of any bird in South America.

2. It is the heaviest flying bird in South America.

3. It is the tallest flying bird in South America.

4. It has the longest tongue of any bird in South America.

5. It has the largest wingspan of any bird in South America.

6. It lives at the highest altitude of any bird in South America.

KING PENGUIN

This is the second-largest species of penguin, and is distinguished by the solid, vivid orange teardrop shape on the sides of its head. Only the emperor penguin is taller than the king penguin. King penguins live and breed away from the Antarctic continent, and are found on some of South America's southernmost coasts.

A B C D

G

E F

- King penguins don't build a nest, but rest their egg on top of their feet to keep it warm. When the newborn chick hatches, they shelter that on their feet, too.

- These penguins are superb swimmers. They dive deep to catch fish.

Which two pieces are not needed to complete the egg?

SCREAMER

The horned screamer is like the unicorn of the bird world! Its white spike is made of cartilage and can be longer than your middle finger.

Cross out any shape that has four sides to find out which countries this bird lives in.

- These birds are huge (around 1 m/3 ft long) and have bony spikes on each wing.

- They are noisy birds, with a variety of honking, trumpeting, and screaming calls. These noises warn other birds of predators, or are used as a greeting or a mating call.

Ecuador

Uruguay

Peru

Chile

Colombia

French Guiana

Bolivia

Brazil

Guyana

Argentina

Suriname

Venezuela

EUROPE

As the world's second-smallest continent, Europe has fewer bird species than most other continents; it has probably between 500 and 800 species. Its relatively mild climate attracts plenty of breeding and migrating birds, making their homes on farmland, in forests, and around its extensive coastline. It is home to some of the world's most common species, including sparrows, starlings, gulls, and swallows.

KINGFISHER

This beautiful, bright bird changes in the light, from glistening green to an electric turquoise shade. It is a shy bird that isn't easy to spot, but if you're lucky you might catch a glimpse of its darting flight along a river.

- A kingfisher cuts through the surface of the water in a V-shape. A third eyelid covers its eyes to protect them from impact with the water.

- When it catches a fish, a kingfisher perches on a branch and hits the fish against it before eating it.

The common kingfisher is found across most of Europe except the far north. It feeds on fish, small crustaceans, and some insects. Fill in the missing numbers and the highlighted square will tell you what percentage of its own body weight a kingfisher has to catch and eat each day.

	+	5	=	22
+		+		+
16	+		=	
=		=		=
	+	27	=	

38

STARLING

Native to Europe, these birds have been introduced to other continents and are now an invasive species in countries such as New Zealand, South Africa, and the US. They form enormous, swirling flocks in the sky at dusk. These flocks move in formation, creating flowing, changing waves. A flock is called a murmuration and can contain tens of thousands of starlings.

It is sometimes said that a fan of one famous writer released birds mentioned in their works into New York City's Central Park—including about a hundred European starlings. Use the decoder to work out which writer they loved so much.

A	E	S	R	O	K	G
B	A	C	P	H	T	N
	1	2	3	4	5	6

A2.B4.B1.A5.A1.A2.B3.A1.B1.A3.A1

SPARROW

The house sparrow is another European bird that was introduced to New York City in the 1800s. They are not only found near houses, but anywhere there are people: farms, restaurants, streets, and also near landfill sites. They feed on seeds but also on scraps of human food.

▪ These clever little birds have been seen activating automatic doors to gain entry into supermarkets, looking for crumbs and treats!

Which one of these sparrows does not look like any of the others?

PUFFIN

The Atlantic puffin is designed for life on the open waves. It has webbed feet and can dive underwater for up to a minute. It uses its wings as paddles, and feet for steering. These birds are also strong, fast flyers but make quite a clumsy crash landing!

Can you find these six characters in the scene?

- Puffins spend most of the year out at sea, far away from land. They return to the coast for the breeding season.

- At sea, they rest on the surface, bobbing around on the swell of the water.

- During breeding, they form large colonies. A breeding pair nests in a burrow or between rocks.

- They feed on small fish and the record they can carry in their bill at one time is 62! 10 or 12 is more normal though.

Draw your own swan reflection scene. Copy the swan here help you.

- This bird is huge, and is one of the heaviest flying birds in the world.

MUTE SWAN

The mute swan is a common swan species, marked out by its orange and black beak. It dabbles this in the water, feeding on plants, insects, worms, and other water creatures. Mute swans are attentive, caring parents and usually have between five and twelve young, called cygnets, each year.

JAY

The Eurasian jay has beautiful plumage, but is shy and not seen very often. Sometimes you might catch a flash of blue or pink as it flies from tree to tree. It has a harsh alarm call, and is also a good mimic, copying the sounds of other birds.

Jays collect and bury acorns which they then find later in the winter when food is scarce. Find the six acorns that the jay has hidden in this grid. Each number shows exactly how many acorns are next to the numbered squares. They can be touching on a side or a corner but no acorn is in a square with a number.

		3		
	1	4		
		4		
		🌰	2	
1				

BACKYARD BIRDS

A variety of birds are comfortable enough around people to pay a visit to domestic homes and gardens.
Many of them can be attracted to food such as seeds, nuts, and fat balls.

How many of each of the species described below can you spot in the scene?

- The pretty wood pigeon is one of the larger birds seen near houses. Listen for their coo-COO-coo sound.

- The great tit is a common sight in Europe's urban areas. It has a stripe going down its yellow breast.

- European robins have a small, round bright orange-red breast.

- Male blackbirds live up to their name, with a glossy black plumage. They have a bright golden beak.

MAGPIE

These birds have a bad reputation for being noisy and for eating the eggs and chicks of other birds. However, they are thought to be one of the cleverest birds.

Use your mega-brain to fill in the missing numbers so that each row, column, and linked set has the numbers 1 to 6. The pink numbers will show you which of the facts below about magpies are true.

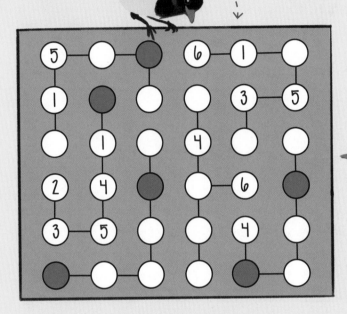

1. An adult magpie's tail makes up at least half of its overall length.

2. Magpies use tools to cut food into correctly sized portions for their young.

3. They play games together and work in teams to achieve better results.

4. When a magpie dies, others gather around to give it a kind of funeral.

5. They are great mimics and can imitate human speech and laughter.

6. For its body size, its brain is the equivalent size and weight as a dolphin's brain.

NIGHTINGALE

With their plain brown upper parts and paler underside, these birds won't grab your attention until they open their beak. They are famous for their song, especially the males, which trill and warble through a glorious range of notes.

Use the code key to find out which European country has the nightingale as its national bird.

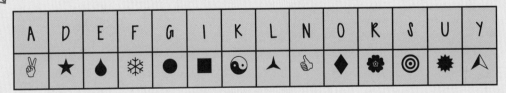

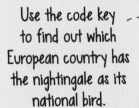

WHITE STORK

This striking bird has long legs for wading, and a long red beak for fishing and catching small creatures such as lizards, toads, scorpions, snakes, and rodents. Its body is white, with black flight feathers. It flies with its long neck and legs outstretched.

They build their nests on top of manmade objects such as houses, chimneys, towers, and tall poles and pylons. Their nests are huge—almost big enough to hold a small car! Spot five differences between these two nesting scenes.

- Both parents help to raise the fledgling chicks.

- Hundreds of thousands of them gather across large areas of Europe and migrate to Africa for the winter.

- They make a noise called bill-clattering, which is said to sound like distant machine gun fire.

SWALLOW

Often known simply as the swallow, the barn swallow is the world's most widespread species of swallow. Their upper feathers have a beautiful glossy, blue sheen. They make a nest of mud, often near to human habitation, and migrate south for the winter.

Which three swallows have flown away in the second picture?

- Swallows are related to swifts and martins. They all have a similar body shape and feeding style, catching insects in midair.

BARN OWL

This is one of the most common and widespread species of owl, and one of the few birds that is found in some part of every continent except Antarctica. Its heart-shaped face helps direct sounds, enabling it to hear the tiny movements in the darkness.

Fill in this grid so that each row, column, and minigrid has one of each of the owl's prey in it.

- The barn owl, like other owls, is an amazing night hunter. Its ears are not level with each other; one side is higher than the other. This gives it even better hearing to judge the distance and position of its prey.

BIRDS OF PREY

Europe has a large number of magnificent birds of prey.

Find all the birds of prey from the list in the wordsearch grid The words can appear up and down, across, or diagonally, and forward or backward.

P	E	R	E	O	S	P	B	U	Z	Z	H	A	R	R	V	K	E	S	R
K	E	S	G	L	S	P	E	R	E	G	R	I	N	E	U	I	D	E	R
A	N	P	I	Y	L	B	A	K	B	Y	S	P	A	R	L	T	L	O	H
G	O	S	E	N	R	E	U	V	E	R	N	N	T	O	T	G	Y	R	R
V	H	A	R	R	I	E	R	Z	U	S	I	E	K	U	A	P	O	P	R
U	K	E	S	T	E	O	M	I	Z	L	T	S	O	E	T	E	R	S	A
L	G	G	O	S	P	R	E	Y	R	K	T	R	Z	O	S	R	H	E	H
T	R	Y	S	Z	A	B	K	E	S	T	I	V	Z	M	S	T	A	H	W
B	I	U	R	Z	E	O	M	D	O	B	O	T	U	E	T	P	R	N	D
G	N	L	K	A	R	H	Y	E	R	U	E	H	B	L	O	V	R	E	N
Y	E	S	I	Z	O	E	O	B	S	Z	G	O	S	I	T	U	A	O	L
R	Z	U	T	Z	W	H	S	S	T	Z	M	S	S	N	R	L	H	G	E
F	L	S	P	A	R	R	O	W	H	A	W	K	T	Y	A	T	R	O	N
A	A	Y	E	F	T	T	R	B	A	R	K	P	I	M	C	U	E	S	O
L	H	Q	V	U	L	T	U	G	B	D	Y	S	H	A	R	K	R	H	G
C	E	S	C	A	S	I	W	A	N	Y	N	O	W	S	W	E	G	A	S
O	Y	I	F	M	W	P	G	R	I	N	E	U	E	Z	Z	A	R	W	A
N	M	E	G	I	N	H	A	C	E	H	O	T	D	I	H	E	R	K	H
B	U	Z	Z	M	E	W	Y	R	H	C	I	H	N	N	Y	N	E	M	O
T	F	E	R	L	I	N	A	S	R	K	L	S	P	A	R	O	W	Y	J

SPARROWHAWK
BUZZARD
KESTREL
HOBBY
FALCON
OSPREY
MERLIN
HARRIER
KITE
GOSHAWK
PEREGRINE
EAGLE
VULTURE

▪ As with all birds of prey, the female sparrowhawk is larger than the male.

▪ A kestrel can often be seen hovering, facing into the wind, while it scours below to see if it can spot small prey.

▪ The red kite soars through the sky above rivers, roads, and fields. Look for its long forked tail, which twists as it changes direction.

▪ A buzzard has broad, rounded wings for soaring. When it's not flying, it can be seen perched on high poles.

WOODPECKERS

Woodpeckers are famous for drilling into tree trunks with their beaks to dig for insects or make a nests. There are over 300 species of woodpecker in the world. The most common species found in Europe are the greater spotted woodpecker and the European green woodpecker.

Match these woodpeckers into identical pairs.

AVOCET

This wading bird has long legs, webbed feet, and a highly unusual bill. It is long and thin, curving upward and can sweep from side to side through the water to find food.

Follow the footprints in the direction they're facing, for the number of steps shown on each. Which of the worms will the avocet end at?

• An avocet feeds mostly on worms and crustaceans. In deeper water, they feed like a duck, tipping their head down and their rear end up, to find food below the surface.

GOLDEN EAGLE

This majestic bird is found across much of Europe, North America, and parts of Asia and north Africa. Golden eagles are most often found in mountainous areas. They hunt in the daytime, often in pairs; one eagle chases their prey toward the other one.

Which of these silhouettes is an exact match for the golden eagle?

- They eat mammals as large as rabbits, as well as reptiles, birds, fish, and carrion.

- A golden eagle is enormous, with a wingspan over 2 m (7 ft). It is such an awesome predator that it is at the top of the food chain.

BEE-EATER

A fantastically bright and attractive bird, it eats all kinds of insects, not only bees. Its long bill is sharp, to keep a tight grip on its prey. Once caught, the insect is carried back to a perch where the bird rubs or thrashes it against a branch to remove any stingers.

Finish this large picture by copying the smaller one below.

- There are many species of bee-eater, but the European bee-eater is one of the brightest.

WATER BIRDS

The rivers, lakes, wetlands, and ponds of Europe are home to a host of water-dwelling birds. Many of them have webbed feet, making them powerful swimmers but clumsy or even unable to walk on land. Lots of them feed on water plants, insects, grubs, crustaceans, and sometimes larger creatures such as lizards.

Study this scene and then turn the page. See how much you can remember!

▪ A moorhen sometimes uses its long, spindly legs and large feet to walk across the water on lilypads.

▪ You might spot a heron standing on the bank, either looking for food, with its neck stretched out, or hunched down with its neck bent over its chest.

▪ A female mallard lays more than half her body weight in eggs during the nesting period. Males and females look very different.

▪ The great crested grebe has elaborate decorations on its head and neck.

▪ A coot has unusual feet, with rounded flaps of skin on its toes which act like webbing.

▪ A male mallard has an iridescent, green-blue head.

▪ Shoveler ducks have similar plumage to mallards, but have a broad, flat, shovel-shaped bill for dabbling.

TEST YOUR MEMORY

How much can you remember from the picture on the previous page?

1. How many herons are flying?
2. Which bird has caught a fish?
3. How many female ducks (with brown plumage) are there?

4. Which two species are on land?
5. Are any of the ducks dabbling?
6. Which bird has chicks following it?

THE TIT FAMILY

Can you complete this jigsaw? Which piece isn't needed?

Some of Europe's most familiar and most-loved birds are species of tit. They include the lovely green and yellow great tit, the blue tit, the distinctive crested tit, and the long-tailed tit.

LAPWING

This bird is common throughout Europe. In English, it is also known as the peewit because of the sound it makes to attract a mate. Lapwings appear black and white, but at a close distance their iridescent green and purple sheen is visible.

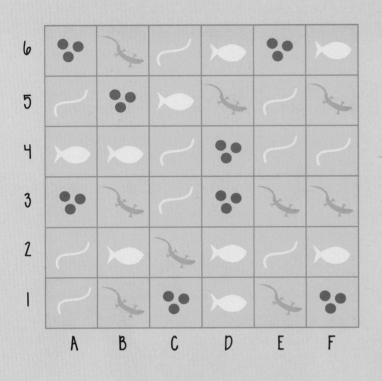

Find out what lapwings like to eat by following the directions through this grid.

Start at C1. Go left 2 squares, up 4 squares, right 4 squares, down 1 square, left 2 squares, and up 2 squares.

Berries
Lizard
Worm
Fish

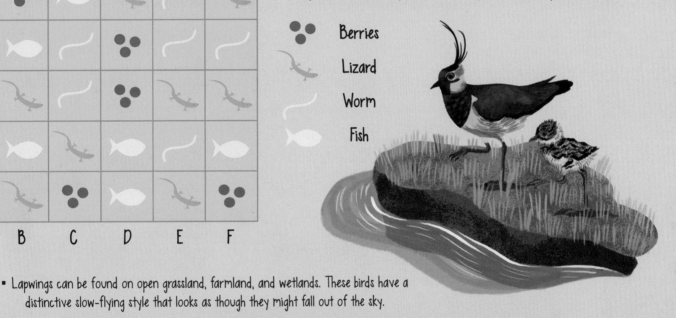

▪ Lapwings can be found on open grassland, farmland, and wetlands. These birds have a distinctive slow-flying style that looks as though they might fall out of the sky.

GOLDEN ORIOLE

This stunning bird is around the size of a blackbird but has much brighter plumage. It is a shy, secretive bird that is rarely seen despite its yellow feathers. It has a distinctive, whistling song, most often heard as the sun rises.

Decode this message to find out what the people of northern Europe predict when they see these birds.

A1.A4.B3 / A6.A1.B2.B5.A1 / A8.B4 / A6.B1.B5.B7.A3.A5

	1	2	3	4	5	6	7	8
A	T	C	N	H	G	S	B	O
B	P	A	E	F	R	D	I	Y

ANTARCTICA

This is a place of records: it is the coldest, windiest, and driest continent on Earth. The air temperature can fall as low as minus 89.4 °C (minus 128.9 °F) but the snow surface temperature can be even lower. Creatures that live here are well adapted to the extreme conditions. Very few birds live on the mainland, but lots of seabirds spend the summer on the surrounding islands.

GREY-HEADED ALBATROSS

Also known as the gray-headed mollymawk, this large seabird makes its nests on isolated islands in the Southern Ocean.

• The grey-headed albatross nest is a tall, mossy mound made of mud.

Which five chicks in the scene still have to be photographed by the scientist?

52

PENGUIN PARADE

Five species of penguin breed in Antarctica, while some other species live on the subantarctic islands nearby.

- Huge numbers of penguins gather in groups called rookeries for breeding every year.

- Adélie rookeries can grow to more than 500,000 birds!

Chinstrap penguins inhabit islands of the Southern Pacific and the Antarctic Oceans. Check out this black-and-white spectacle of chinstrap penguins. Can you spot a sneaky pooch hiding in the crowd?

ROCKHOPPER PENGUIN

This bird doesn't venture onto the Antarctic mainland, but breeds on nearby islands. They are also found on some South American islands, in Chile, and New Zealand, making them the most widely-distributed penguin species.

Follow the step by step instructions to draw your very own rockhopper penguin.

• They move around on land by jumping across the rocks, rather than waddling—which is where their name originates.

1

2

3

SKUA

This huge seabird is a bird bully. It attacks other birds to steal their food. It isn't afraid to dive-bomb gulls, boobies, and shearwaters, forcing them to regurgitate food they have swallowed or stored. They will also attack the nesting sites of Adélie penguins to grab their chicks and eggs.

Which silhouette is an exact outline of the picture of the South Polar skua?

A

B

C

D

E

EMPEROR PENGUIN

The Antarctic is a harsh place to live. Most animals leave for the winter, but the emperor penguin stays to breed on the sea ice that surrounds the continent. They survive the harsh conditions by huddling in groups that can contain 5,000 or more adults.

Each adult has just a single chick to care for. Are there equal numbers of adults and chicks in this scene?

▪ The female lays her egg and then transfers it to the male. She treks for miles to reach the ocean and feed for the first time in months.

▪ After the egg has hatched, the female returns with a belly full of fish, which she regurgitates to feed the chick.

▪ The male keeps the egg off the ice by resting it on top of his feet. He covers it with a brood pouch to keep it warm.

AFRICA

Africa is famous for its wildlife and safaris, and its birds do not disappoint. From the iconic ostrich and the talented weaverbirds to the striking, stamping secretary bird, it has an array of wonderful species making their homes in its deserts, savannahs, lakes, and mountains.

OSTRICH

The tallest and heaviest bird in the world, these creatures really are astounding. They are much taller than a person—even a tall basketball player! They have tiny wings and cannot fly, but can run exceptionally fast, even over long distances.

How quickly could an ostrich run a marathon? Cross out all the multiples of 2, 7, and 10 to find out roughly how many minutes it would take.

100

30

90

20

70

60

60

35

24

49

36

21

45

• Its long, powerful legs are strong enough to deliver a mighty kick. It uses them to protect itself from predators, even lions.

• They lay their huge eggs in a nest, which is a hollow scraped in the ground. Each egg can weigh as much as 24 chicken eggs!

• They are the only birds with two toes on each foot.

WEAVERBIRD

There are many species of weaverbirds in Africa. The southern masked weaver is widespread and has bright yellow plumage, a black face, and red eyes. It is famous for its nest-building skills.

Can you spot five differences between these two pictures?

- The males make their nests from reeds, grass, and leaves, intricately woven into shape, to attract a mate. The female then lines the nest with soft grass and feathers.

- Their hanging nest, often with a narrow, tube-shaped entrance, helps keep them safe from lizards, crows, snakes, and birds of prey.

SHOEBILL

Named for its enormous beak, this bird looks prehistoric. It is tall, reaching 1.4 m (4.5 ft), with a sturdy body and broad wings. Its shoe-shaped bill is razor sharp, with a curved hook at the very tip. It feeds on fish and snakes but will also tackle baby crocodiles!

▪ It generally lives alone, only getting together with another bird for mating.

23
22
18
9
35
27
16

It flaps its wings more slowly than most birds. Add up the numbers on the flowers to find out how many flaps it makes per minute.

SECRETARY BIRD

This distinctive bird has the longest legs of any bird of prey!

It features on the South African coat of arms and is the national bird of another African country. Cross out any letters that appear twice or more to find out which country.

▪ Secretary birds are unusual because they mostly hunt on foot instead of in the air. They kill with their feet, stomping on the prey and then holding it down to tear it apart with their strong bills.

L   M   O
H
R   O
T   Z
O   H
G   D   Z
S   I
C   U   G
R   M
O   C   I   T   L   N
A
O

WHYDAH

The pin-tailed whydah is a small songbird, found in much of Africa, south of the Sahara Desert. It generally has a bright reddish-orange bill and feeds on grains, seeds, and insects.

At times, the males and females look similar, but a breeding male's plumage changes to a striking black and white on its head and body. It also grows extravagant extra feathers; join the dots here to find out what it looks like during breeding season.

▪ These additional feathers can grow up to 20 cm (8 in) long. After breeding, the male loses these long feathers.

▪ These birds are "brood parasites" like the common cuckoo. They don't raise their own young, but add their eggs to the nest of other birds and let those birds feed and care for the whydah chicks with their own.

- A vulture's stomach has high levels of acid to digest rotting meat quickly.

VULTURE

Africa has eleven species of vulture. They generally have bald heads and necks, which lets them feast on a carcass without getting messy feathers.

Vultures play a very important role in keeping the landscape clear of carrion. Solve the number equation to find out what percentage of Africa's dead creatures are cleared away by vultures. Start on the left and follow the arrows.

$100 \div$

$4 +$

$7 \times$

$10 +$

$30 \div$

$5 = ?$

TURACO

There are several turaco species found in Africa. The largest is the great blue turaco, which has brilliant blue plumage in both the males and females.

- Turacos have unique pigments that give them their bright blue, green, and red feathers (depending upon their species).

- Turacos are related to another African bird called the go-away bird. Its call sounds as if it is shouting "kay-waaaay" as a warning. They have much more dull plumage than many turacos.

Both turacos and go-away birds are members of the Musophagidae family. The name comes from one of their most common foods. Fill in the code key and use it to find out what this name actually means.

A	O		N	B
B	P		O	C
C	Q		P	D
D	R		Q	E
E	S		R	F
F	T		S	G
G	U		T	H
H	V		U	I
I	W		V	J
J	X		W	K
K	Y		X	L
L	Z		Y	M
M	A		Z	N

Coded message is:

NMZMZM QMFQD

FLAMINGO

There are six species of flamingo in the world, and the greater flamingo which lives in Africa and Asia is the largest and most widespread. They are very distinctive, with long legs, curved necks, pink plumage, and black and pink hooked bills.

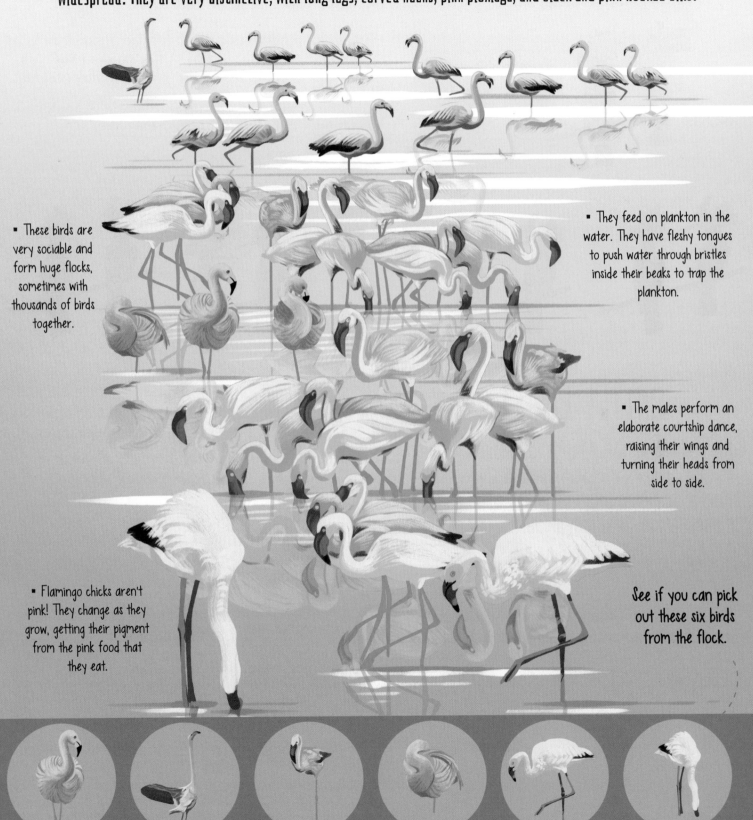

- These birds are very sociable and form huge flocks, sometimes with thousands of birds together.

- They feed on plankton in the water. They have fleshy tongues to push water through bristles inside their beaks to trap the plankton.

- The males perform an elaborate courtship dance, raising their wings and turning their heads from side to side.

- Flamingo chicks aren't pink! They change as they grow, getting their pigment from the pink food that they eat.

See if you can pick out these six birds from the flock.

HOOPOE

These distinctive birds are about the size of a starling. They get their name from their repeated "hoo–poo" call. They are usually seen singly or in pairs, and they mate with just one partner each season.

Which of the silhouettes is not an exact match for this pair of birds?

- The bird uses its long, strong beak to poke into the ground looking for insects. It can be seen bashing these insects around to remove the wings and legs before eating them!

- Females and young hoopoes can give off a nasty stench to keep predators away.

A

B

C

D

E

CATTLE EGRET

Native to Africa, these small herons are now found on most continents. They are often seen around livestock, as the hooves of the animals disturb the grubs and insects that the egrets feed on. Unlike many herons, they tend to keep away from water.

The birds don't only associate with cattle. Unscramble these groups of letters to find the names of several other large animals they follow around.

AUFLOBF

BRAZE

FERGIFA

TOPSMUPHIPOA

MARABOU STORK

This bird won't win any beauty contests! But it does play an important role in clearing carrion and rubbish, as it hangs around waste dumps and scavenges kills from other predators.

Search the trash to see if you can find:

2 hats

3 fish skeletons

4 drinks cans

5 shoes

- It is an enormous bird, with a wingspan equivalent to two people end to end. It grows to around 1.5 m (5 ft) tall.

DRONGO

This clever bird is found in South Africa's Kalahari Desert, where it follows meerkats and small birds to steal their food. It tricks them by mimicking alarm calls that send them scurrying for cover, leaving any tasty treats they had unearthed for the drongos to grab for themselves.

- Drongos are so clever that if one alarm call stops being effective, they switch to make the alarm call of a different creature.

Work out which meerkat is the oldest, down to the youngest, using the clues.

1. The oldest is not on either end.

2. The youngest is in between the second and third oldest.

3. The fourth oldest is on the left, but not next to the oldest.

4. The third oldest is the farthest away from the fourth oldest.

HONEYGUIDE

The greater honeyguide has a notable habit. It loves to raid bees' nests for beeswax and larvae, but has learned to guide humans to hidden nests where they smoke out the bees, and make it much safer for the birds to raid.

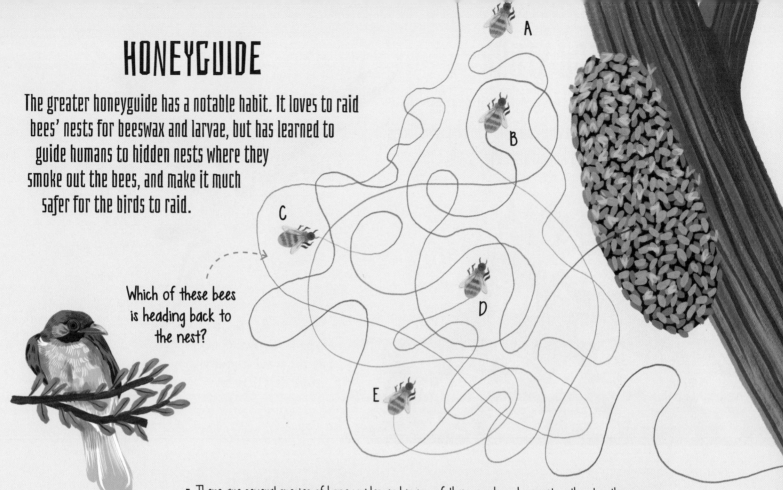

Which of these bees is heading back to the nest?

▪ There are several species of honeyguides and many of them are brood parasites; they lay their eggs in the nest of another species of bird. The honeyguide chicks can be vicious. Once hatched, they attack and kill the other, smaller chicks so the parents have only one hungry mouth to feed.

SKIMMER

The African skimmer is a seabird, found on the coast but also seen flying over rivers such as the Nile and the Congo. The lower part of its beak is longer than the upper part, and is used to scoop fish out of the water as the skimmer flies along the surface.

Which of these skimmers does not match another one in the flock?

OXPECKER

There are two species of oxpecker in Africa: the red-billed and the yellow-billed. Both of them are found climbing over the body of large animals, pecking up parasites such as ticks and mites. Sometimes, they peck at a bleeding wound to drink the blood.

See if you can work out which 6 animals these oxpeckers are pecking.

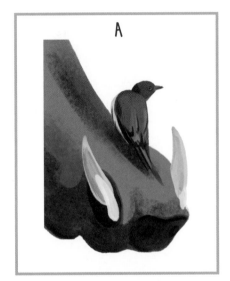

A

HAWRTORG

- - - - - - - - - - - - - - - - - - - -

B

SHOCKEIORNS

- - - - - - - - - - - - - - - - - - - -

C

REFIGAF

- - - - - - - - - - - - - - - - - - - -

D

BEZRA

- - - - - - - - - - - - - - - - - - - -

E

SUPTAHOPIMPO

- - - - - - - - - - - - - - - - - - - -

F

FOALFUB

- - - - - - - - - - - - - - - - - - - -

SCOPS OWL

Like all owls, the African scops owl has a round face with forward-facing eyes that helps it judge distances for hunting. These eyes don't move around in the sockets; instead, the owl is able to rotate its head up to 270 degrees.

Many owls, including the scops owl, are nocturnal, hunting at night. Search in the grid for all kinds of creatures that they hunt for. The words can appear up and down, across, or diagonally, and forward or backward.

GRASSHOPPER
BEETLE
MOTH
CRICKET
SPIDER
SCORPION
GECKO
BIRD
RABBIT
MOUSE

M	A	C	B	R	M	M	O	U	S	E	A
M	O	P	H	I	O	A	N	R	G	B	B
O	N	H	C	C	T	G	E	D	R	E	B
U	G	R	A	R	R	D	S	B	A	E	T
L	E	A	B	I	I	S	C	E	S	T	D
I	C	R	X	P	H	C	O	E	S	L	G
T	K	L	S	C	O	O	K	T	J	E	E
M	O	U	S	S	E	R	P	E	O	Y	C
B	E	E	T	L	A	P	O	P	T	E	K
T	I	R	A	B	B	I	T	U	A	O	D
G	R	A	S	S	H	O	P	P	E	R	X
S	C	O	R	L	S	N	I	Y	I	O	C
L	L	S	M	O	T	H	M	B	U	T	O

KORI BUSTARD

The kori bustard is huge. It is Africa's largest flying bird. However, it prefers to stay on the ground where possible, as flying isn't easy for a bird of this size. It can often be seen among grazing animals, where it feeds on the insects that are disturbed by the larger animals.

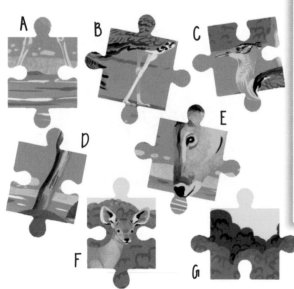

A B C
D E
F G

Which of the puzzle pieces is not needed to finish the picture?

GUINEA FOWL

These distinctive birds are common in sub-Saharan Africa. They have amazing spotted plumage and a dinosaur-like casque, or head crest.

Fill in the number grid and use the highlighted circles to discover which of the facts below are true. The numbers 1 to 5 should appear once each in every row, column, and set of connected circles.

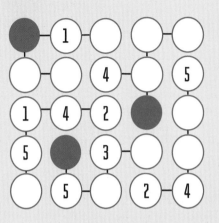

1. The mothers have only two or three babies and take great care of them.

2. The babies are called keets, not chicks.

3. They mostly feed at night.

4. They are sometimes kept as watchdogs to keep predators away.

5. They sometimes follow groups of monkeys to gather up dropped fruit.

RED-BILLED QUELEA

This is another type of weaverbird that is found in huge flocks across sub-Saharan Africa. A single flock may have tens of thousands, sometimes millions, of birds.

Use the decoder on the right to find out an amazing fact about these birds.

_ _ _ _ _ _ _ _ _ _ _ _ _ _ _ _ _ _

24.12.9.22.9 / 5.22.9 / 17.19.22.9 /
19.10 / 24.12.9.17 / 24.12.5.18 / 5.18.3 /
19.24.12.9.22 / 1.13.16.8 / 1.13.16.8 /
6.13.22.8 / 13.18 / 24.12.9 / 1.19.22.16.8

_ _ _ _ _ _ _ _ _ _ _ _ _ _ _ _

_ _ _ _ _ _ _ _ _ _ _ _ _ _ _ _ _ _

A	5		N	18
B	6		O	19
C	7		P	20
D	8		Q	21
E	9		R	22
F	10		S	23
G	11		T	24
H	12		U	25
I	13		V	26
J	14		W	1
K	15		X	2
L	16		Y	3
M	17		Z	4

ASIA

This vast continent is the biggest of all the continents, and so it has a huge variety of habitats for birds to live in. They include woodlands, grasslands, wetlands, coasts, rain forests, mountains, and both hot and cold deserts.

RED-CROWNED CRANE

The second-rarest crane species in the world, this magnificent bird lives in wetlands in various parts of the continent.

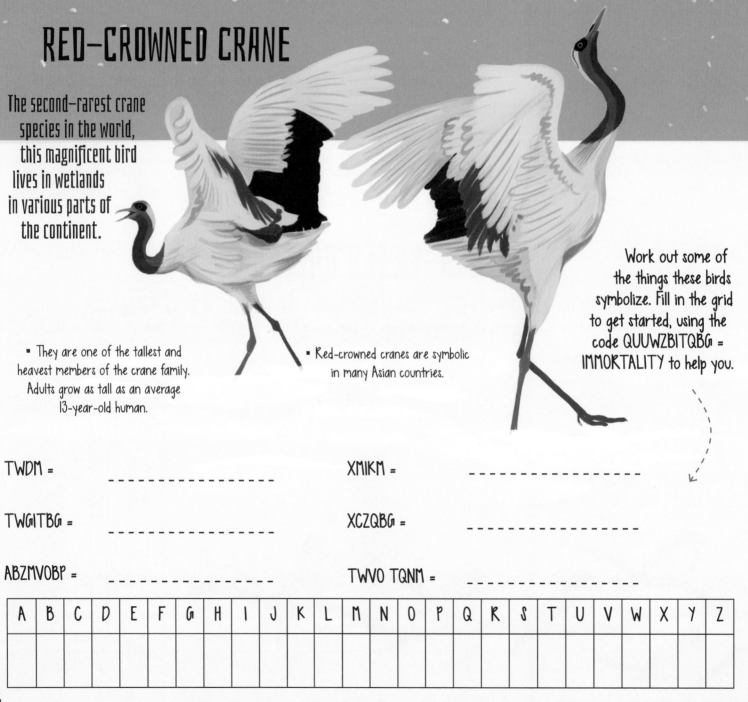

- They are one of the tallest and heavest members of the crane family. Adults grow as tall as an average 13-year-old human.

- Red-crowned cranes are symbolic in many Asian countries.

Work out some of the things these birds symbolize. Fill in the grid to get started, using the code QUUWZBITQBG = IMMORTALITY to help you.

TWDM = _ _ _ _ _ _ _ _ _ _ _ _ _ _ _ _

XMIKM = _ _ _ _ _ _ _ _ _ _ _ _ _ _ _ _

TWGITBG = _ _ _ _ _ _ _ _ _ _ _ _ _ _ _ _

XCZQBG = _ _ _ _ _ _ _ _ _ _ _ _ _ _ _

ABZMVOBP = _ _ _ _ _ _ _ _ _ _ _ _ _ _ _

TWVO TQNM = _ _ _ _ _ _ _ _ _ _ _ _ _ _

A	B	C	D	E	F	G	H	I	J	K	L	M	N	O	P	Q	R	S	T	U	V	W	X	Y	Z

PITTA

There are around 30 species of pitta, many with brilliant plumage. They are sometimes nicknamed "jewels of the forest." Some are found in Africa and Australia but many live in southeast Asia and India.

Pair up each of these beautiful birds. Which one isn't part of a pair?

- Hunting, capture, and trade of these birds is against the law.

A B C D E F G H I

COMMON PHEASANT

This bird has been taken from Asia and introduced in many other parts of the world.

- Males have golden body feathers with a green neck and red face. In comparison, females have less elaborate brown plumage.

Pheasants are often hunted as game birds. Help this pair find a way around this field to avoid the hunters. Join the dots to make one continuous, looped line. Not all the dots have to be joined, but each number shows how many lines surround it. Some lines are there to help you.

3	3	2	2	3
2	1	2	2	2
2	2	3	2	3
2	1	1	2	1
3	1	2	3	3

PEAFOWL

A member of the pheasant family, this bird is often called a peacock, which is the name of the male. He is known for his splendid tail, which fans out to show off the beautiful stiff feathers during courtship displays.

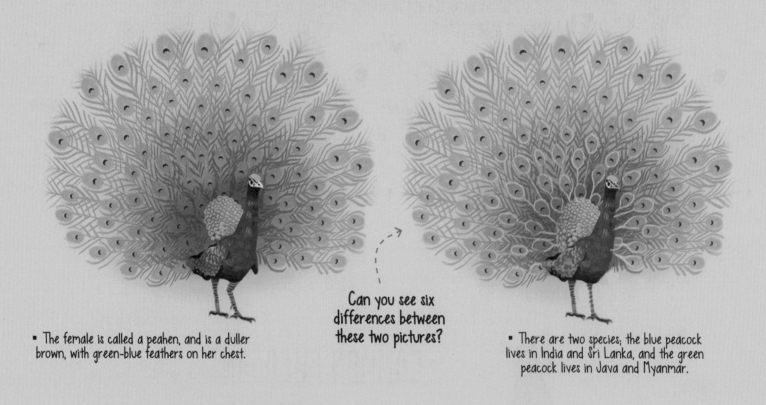

Can you see six differences between these two pictures?

- The female is called a peahen, and is a duller brown, with green-blue feathers on her chest.

- There are two species; the blue peacock lives in India and Sri Lanka, and the green peacock lives in Java and Myanmar.

GREAT CORMORANT

These majestic birds are famous for their fishing skills, and for standing with their wings outstretched to dry off after they leave the water.

Cross out all the letters that appear twice. The ones that are left spell the ancient Japanese method of fishing using trained cormorants.

COMMON CUCKOO

These birds spend their summers in Asia or Europe, and migrate to Africa for the winter. The females famously lay their egg in the nest of another bird. When the chick hatches, it pushes all the other eggs or chicks out of the nest, meaning it gets all the food from its foster parents.

- Their name comes from the noise they make, but they only call like this during breeding season.

One of these cheeky cuckoos is the real mother of the chick being fed. Find out which it is by counting her breast stripes. She has an odd, not an even, number.

A

B

C

D

E

KINGFISHER

This is an oriental dwarf kingfisher. It is only as long as your outstretched hand. Its plumage is astonishing.

Use the key to help you finish the picture, showing all of its glorious, vivid feathers.

1=

2=

3=

4=

5=

6=

7=

8=

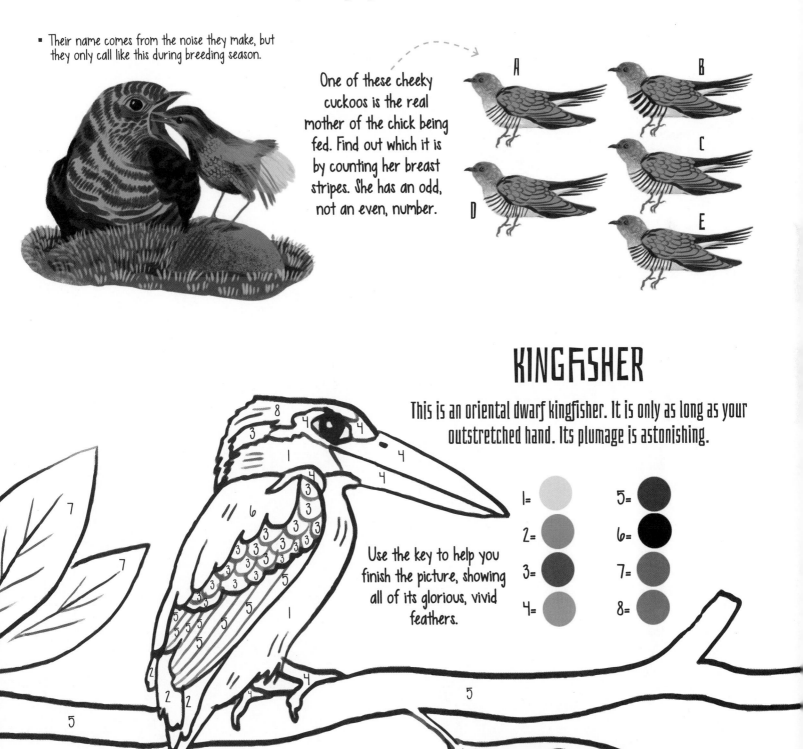

MANDARIN DUCK

These distinctive ducks originally come from China, Japan, North Korea, South Korea, and parts of Russia. Humans have introduced them to Europe and North America. They are omnivores that eat plants and small creatures.

How many words of three or more letters can you make out of this duck's name?

MANDARIN DUCK

- - - - - - - - - - - - - -

- - - - - - - - - - - - - -

- - - - - - - - - - - - - -

- - - - - - - - - - - - - -

■ They are classed as perching ducks because they make their nests in holes in trees. When the ducklings hatch, they jump down to the ground from the nest. They can't fly until they are a few weeks old.

LITTLE EGRET

A member of the heron family, this bird has white plumage, black legs, and yellow feet. It has long white plumes on its head and neck during the breeding season.

It has a patch of bare skin between its eyes and its beak. Follow the arrows starting from the top left triangle to find out what shade this patch changes to in the breeding season.

■ It uses its long legs for wading and its large feet to kick up food from the shallows.

MAGPIE

There are several species of magpie in Asia. One of the brightest is the common green magpie which has long legs, eyes that are bright red, and a thick black stripe that looks like a mask over its eyes.

Not all common green magpies are green! Some have blue-turquoise wing feathers. Draw the correct bird in the box to complete the pattern.

SNOWY OWL

Snowy owls live in the Arctic regions of Asia (Siberia) and west across Europe and North America. Adult females are white with dark spots and stripes, but adult males are almost pure white.

▪ In many areas, lemmings are the main prey of a snowy owl. However, they also hunt for grouse, ptarmigan, sea ducks, and a variety of small mammals.

lemming

Fill in this grid so there is one of each creature in every row, column, and minigrid.

sea duck

grouse

ptarmigan

HORNBILL

Not all hornbills are found in Asia; some species live in Africa.

• After mating, the female will hide in a hole in a tree. The male seals the hole and just leaves a small slit, big enough for him to deliver food through. This makes the eggs and chicks inside the nest safe from predators.

Use the code grid to find out what the male uses to block up the hole.

CODE
C2.B1.A2 / B3.C4.A2 / A2.B1.C4.D2

	1	2	3	4
A	P	D	I	L
B	U	E	A	W
C	R	M	O	N
D	F	G	K	T

SPOONBILL

The Eurasian spoonbill is found across Central Asia to northeastern China, and from India to the Red Sea. It has mostly white plumage, with a yellow collar during the breeding season. It sweeps its unusually shaped beak from side to side in the water to catch food.

How many of these spoonbills are standing on one leg? Is that more than those standing on two legs?

MALEO

This bird is found only in Indonesia and is about the size of a chicken. However, its eggs are much, much bigger—five times the size of a chicken egg. The female lays her eggs in a hole in the sand, then buries them.

- The sand is warmed by the sun, and this heat incubates the eggs. The parents have nothing to do with it—they wander off and leave their eggs alone. After several weeks, the chicks hatch and have to fend for themselves straightaway.

- Some maleo live in more mountainous areas, and use geothermal heat from hot springs to incubate their eggs.

SAFE   SAFE   SAFE

The newborn chicks have to dig their way out of the sand to reach the surface. They can fly and find food only hours after hatching. However, they must be wary of predators. Find out which of these chicks emerges to a safe space, and which need to be very afraid!

A   B   C   D   E   F

OCEANIA

This southern continent consists of Australia, New Zealand, and lots of other islands in the Pacific. These places are home to many species that exist only in that part of the world.

EMU

Members of the ratite family (the same family as ostriches, rheas, and cassowaries), emus are huge, flightless birds. Their feathers are fluffy and don't form a smooth, flat surface like the feathers of many other birds.

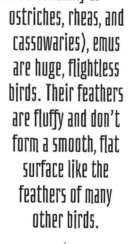

How much do you know about this Australian icon? Answer True or False each time.

They easily grow to be taller than an adult human.   T / F

Its long, long legs allow it to run fast, reaching speeds around 50 km/h (30 mph).   T / F

Emu eggs are bright blue.   T / F

An emu has two or three chicks in one brood.   T / F

Emu chicks stay with their father when they are young.   T / F

Emus love water and are good swimmers.   T / F

Emus have to eat every day to survive.   T / F

KAKAPO

Here's another unusual flightless bird. This one is not from Australia, but from New Zealand. It is a rare parrot that lives on the forest floor and searches for food at night.

Help this kakapo through the maze, avoiding the predators.

START

- It is listed as critically endangered, with not many more than 100 left in the wild.

- Although it can't fly, it is excellent at climbing trees.

- It is the heaviest parrot in the world.

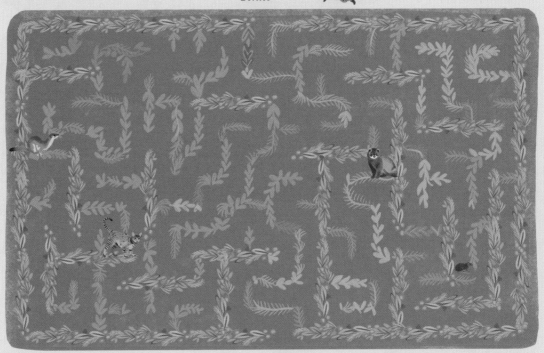

FINISH

GOULDIAN FINCH

These small Australian birds live in eucalyptus trees. Their markings come in a variety of shades.

Which bird doesn't have an exact match?

FROGMOUTH

These birds are found in Australia and southeast Asia. They have amazing camouflage. They blend in so well with the trees, they are almost invisible.

A

B

C

D

E

Which of the puzzle pieces complete the picture?

- They hunt at night for moths, spiders, slugs, snails, beetles, wasps, scorpions, and frogs.

KOOKABURRA

Known for their laughter-like call, this bird is the largest member of the kingfisher family. They hunt by perching on a branch and then flying down to grab their prey in their large beaks.

Cross out all the letters D, E, F, and G that you see here. The remaining letters spell an Aussie nickname for the kookaburra.

B E D U S G H G F A S
D   G N
    D   F   F   M
             G
                F   N
                         E
    C L D E O   F
    C   D O F D C   G
       D   E   G D K G

BOWERBIRD

There are several species of bowerbird, but all of them are known for the way they attract a mate. The male builds a structure and decorates it with a carefully chosen collection of bright objects.

This male satin bowerbird has built his display but another male has stolen some objects in the second picture. The proud builder rearranges them until he's happy once more. Which three objects are missing in the second picture?

LYREBIRD

Two species of lyrebird are found in Australia. Both live on the ground and have a majestic tail that fans out to attract a mate. They are famous for their ability to copy all kinds of sounds, from other birds and even koalas.

LORIKEET

These bright birds are a glorious sight, with their rainbow feathers and orange beaks. They are often seen in pairs. They feed and roost in the trees and are very noisy around sunset.

Which of the lorikeet feathers is slightly different from the others?

▪ The rainbow lorikeet has a special brush on the end of its tongue for sipping nectar from flowers.

BIRD OF PARADISE

There are numerous birds in the Paradisaeidae, or bird of paradise family. Most are found in New Guinea but some also live in Australia.

How many words can you make using the letters in BIRD OF PARADISE?

BIRD OF PARADISE

▪ Males often have two extremely long, trailing tail feathers. They may do an elaborate mating dance to try to attract females for breeding.

BLACK AND WHITE

Not all birds show off with bright patterns. Many stick to the basics of black and white.

- The crest of this cockatoo is bright yellow.

Finish this picture using the the descriptions to help you.

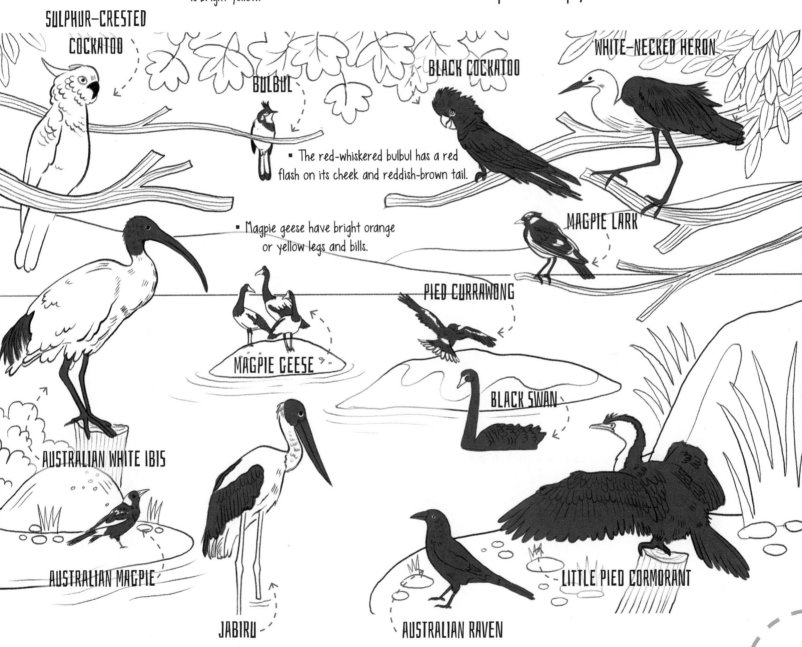

SULPHUR-CRESTED COCKATOO

BULBUL

- The red-whiskered bulbul has a red flash on its cheek and reddish-brown tail.

BLACK COCKATOO

WHITE-NECKED HERON

- Magpie geese have bright orange or yellow legs and bills.

MAGPIE LARK

PIED CURRAWONG

MAGPIE GEESE

BLACK SWAN

AUSTRALIAN WHITE IBIS

AUSTRALIAN MAGPIE

LITTLE PIED CORMORANT

JABIRU

AUSTRALIAN RAVEN

- The jabiru, or black-necked stork, is the only stork in Australia. Its neck is a glossy dark green and purple.

- Black swans are mostly black but have a red bill. They aren't found in the wild anywhere outside Australia.

EAGLE

The wedge-tailed eagle is Australia's largest bird of prey. It eats a lot of carrion (creatures that are already dead). However, if it hunts, it often preys on rabbits and hares.

1				
			1	
		4	4	3
	2			
				2

Work out where the rabbits are hiding in this grid. Each number shows how many rabbits touch that square. They can be touching up, down, sideways, or diagonally. For example, a 2 shows that two of the touching squares have a rabbit in them.

- This eagle is huge, with a 1 m (3 ft) long body and a wingspan up to 2.5 m (8.2 ft).

KIWI

With fluffy feathers that are like fur, wings that are too tiny for flying, and strong, muscular legs, the kiwi is an unusual kind of bird. This ground-dwelling creature lives only in New Zealand, a country that is famous for its many flightless birds.

A kiwi is about the same size as a chicken, but has the largest egg (compared to its body size) of any bird. Solve the puzzle to find out how many times larger its eggs are than a chicken egg.

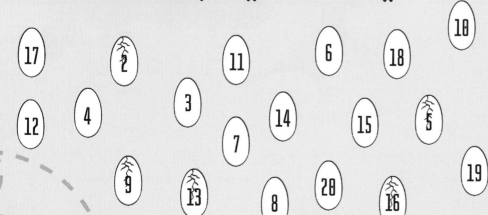

17 2 11 6 18 10 1

12 4 3 14 15 5 19

9 7 13 8 20 16

Cross out all the prime numbers.

Remove eggs that are multiples of 4.

Delete any egg with a 1 on it.

Get rid of the eggs with cracks in.

82

GALAH

This striking bird is a type of cockatoo, but with very distinctive feathers. It gathers in huge flocks, often in shrubs and trees.

See if you can spot six differences between these two pictures.

- It can make the crest feathers on its head stand up. When not erect, the feathers look like a cap or hat.

- They are acrobatic birds that can hang upside down, holding on with one foot.

WEEBILL

With a call that sounds as if it is saying its own name, these birds hunt in flocks. Their feathers range from brown and cream to bright yellow. They feed on insects and weave a neat nest with a narrow entrance at the top.

8.14.26.15.15.22.8.7 / 25.18.9.23 / 18.13 / 26.6.8.7.9.26.15.18.26

Crack the code to find out this bird's claim to fame. First, fill in the grid if 26.6.8.7.9.26.15.18.26 = AUSTRALIA. Work out the letters for the other numbers, then decode the message.

1	2	3	4	5	6	7	8	9	10	11	12	13

14	15	16	27	18	19	20	21	22	23	24	25	26

CASSOWARY

This bird is huge and very distinctive. It has a bright blue head and neck, a red neck wattle, and a large horny head crest called a casque. The cassowary can be over 1. 8 m (6 ft) tall! Its large, clawed feet can deliver a nasty kick if it feels under threat.

- There are three species of cassowary. The Northern cassowary and dwarf cassowary are found only in New Guinea, while the Southern cassowary lives in Australia, too.

- The mother lays her eggs and then moves on, leaving the male to incubate the eggs and look after the hatchlings, often until they are nine months old.

- They are important to the Australian ecosystem because they spread the seeds of so many plants.

Can you find these three small squares somewhere in the main picture?

LITTLE PENGUIN

Native to Australia and New Zealand, the appropriately named little penguin is the smallest species of penguin on Earth. They only reach around 30 cm (1 ft) tall and their beaks are smaller than your little finger.

Figure out the missing number on each of the last two eggs. These will reveal two more names that are sometimes given to the little penguin.

1. Pixie penguin
2. Fairy penguin
3. Pygmy penguin
4. Blue penguin
5. Diving penguin

5	3
1	6

2	6
6	1

7	1
4	3

5	5
1	

4	5
4	

- These penguins live on sandy or rocky shores rather than in icy places.

BUDGERIGAR

These birds are native to Australia but are well known as pets around the world. They are a type of parrot, and use their strong beaks to eat seeds, nuts, and grains. Large flocks of them gather, often near water, when they land at the edge to drink.

Captive-bred budgerigars have a wide range of patterns and shades. However, in the wild, they all look very similar. Use the clues to work out which one of these is the wild budgerigar.

1. It is not purple
2. It is not sitting at either end of the branch
3. It is facing left

MOREPORK

This spotted owl lives in parts of New Zealand. Its name comes from its two-part call, and it has lots of nicknames that sound like its hooting noises. It is one of the continent's smallest owls.

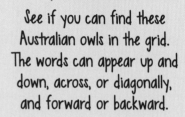

B	A	P	O	W	E	R	F	U	L	E	M	R	B	P
S	O	O	T	Y	R	U	F	B	A	M	O	W	O	U
B	O	O	A	A	R	K	N	A	D	A	R	B	O	H
M	O	R	E	P	O	R	K	R	O	S	E	F	B	A
A	S	O	T	Y	D	U	B	K	Q	K	V	O	O	M
S	L	G	R	A	S	S	S	I	D	E	C	U	O	R
P	O	R	K	C	T	J	O	N	W	D	E	S	K	I
K	R	U	F	O	U	S	O	G	E	S	B	B	R	A

See if you can find these Australian owls in the grid. The words can appear up and down, across, or diagonally, and forward or backward.

- Like other owls, the morepork is sometimes mobbed by smaller birds while it sleeps in the daytime.

- The powerful owl is the largest owl in Australia. It preys on possums and flying foxes.

BARKING   MOREPORK
RUFOUS   GRASS
POWERFUL   MASKED
BOOBOOK   SOOTY

TAKAHE

These New Zealand birds can't fly. They wander around eating tough vegetation with their strong beaks. However, they do have a few surprises in store, not least their astonishing blue, turquoise, and green feathers and brilliant red beaks and legs.

- Their diet of tough grass and roots means that their droppings come out as long sausage shapes. They can poop up to 8 m (26 ft) of these droppings each day!

Cross out any poopy letter W, L, or R. The remaining letters will spell the takahe's major predator.

KEA

This bird is highly unusual. The world's only mountain parrot, it feeds on nectar, seeds, fruits, buds, and insects and their larvae. It digs in the ground with its strong beak to find these grubs.

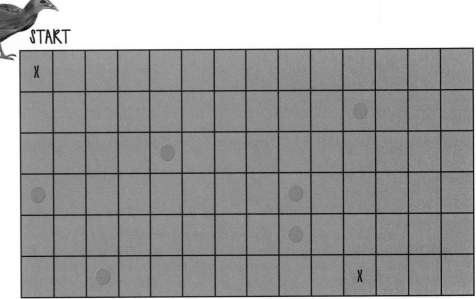

A

B

- When flying, they reveal a bright orange underside on each wing.

- They are famous for being nosy and mischievous. They often gather in tourist areas, sometimes stealing small items, poking around backpacks, and even pecking at car windows and door seals.

They are very clever birds, using tools and working out how to solve problems. Put your bird brain to the test here. If the kea turns the bottom wheel clockwise, will the seeds fall into bowl A or bowl B?

WEKA

Another of the continent's flightless birds, these medium-sized brown birds are also from New Zealand. They are sometimes known as the Maori hen or woodhen.

- These birds are chunky, about the size of a chicken.

Where's the weka? Follow the arrows, one square at a time, to help the weka find its mate. How many of the berries does it eat along the way?

START

X

X

FINISH

ANSWERS

PAGE 4

A = 4 (pheasant)

B = 3 (kingfisher)

C = 5 (scarlet macaw)

D = 2 (peacock)

E = 1 (ostrich)

Pelican =

Flamingo =

Puffin =

Hummingbird =

Toucan =

PAGE 5

8 x 5 = 40

40% of a bird's weight is made up of flight muscles.

PAGE 6

Largest wingspan: Wandering albatross

Smallest wingspan: Bee hummingbird

Highest flying bird: Griffon vulture

Fastest beating wings: Ruby-throated hummingbird

Longest time in the air: Common swift

Heaviest flying bird: Bustard

Longest migration: Arctic tern

PAGE 7

Kiwi = New Zealand

Rhea = South America

Cassowary = New Guinea and Australia

Emu = Australia

Ostrich = Africa

Emperor penguin = Antarctica

PAGE 8

The bird is called a RINGED PLOVER

PAGE 9

PAGE 10

The name of a bird that doesn't migrate is RESIDENT.

T	B	F	R	O	G	L	M	D	C
A	H	D	O	R	M	L	R	S	H
D	L	G	M	O	S	I	C	C	I
R	L	D	I	A	B	W	H	O	C
O	I	G	R	N	D	T	I	U	K
A	W	E	U	M	R	I	C	F	S
D	R	S	N	O	I	C	K	T	T
K	O	R	N	U	B	H	A	I	M
U	O	V	E	T	G	I	D	N	O
N	S	D	E	H	N	V	E	G	V
N	P	F	S	W	I	S	E	F	E
E	C	R	U	N	M	O	D	O	E
R	F	R	O	G	M	O	U	T	H
S	W	G	C	S	U	R	S	R	C
L	R	N	O	G	H	T	I	A	H
S	N	I	G	H	T	H	A	W	K

PAGE 11

Puzzle piece C is not needed to finish the picture.

PAGE 12

Another item on a hummingbird's menu: INSECTS

PAGE 13

D does not have a matching silhouette.

The meadowlark is the state bird for these states: MONTANA, OREGON, WYOMING, KANSAS, NEBRASKA, and NORTH DAKOTA

PAGE 14

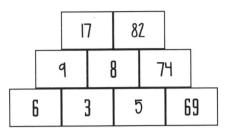

	17	82	
	9	8	74
6	3	5	69

1782 is the year the bald eagle became the USA's national symbol.

There are 15 fish.

PAGE 15

FOOD CACHE is the special name for a storage space.

PAGE 16

A has stolen a sandwich.
B has stolen an apple core.
C has stolen a burger.

PAGE 17

1. Stoop
2. Bats
3. 320 km/h (200 mph)
4. On cliffs
5. Pesticides

PAGE 18

The name of the woodpecker is PILEATED WOODPECKER.

Male American goldfinches are yellow only IN THE SPRING AND SUMMER.

PAGE 19

There are 10 babies

They need to visit the tunnels in this order: D, C, B, A

PAGE 20

PAGE 21

Puzzle pieces A and D are not needed to complete the picture.

PAGE 22

Facts 1, 2, and 4 are true.

PAGE 23

This bird is called PARADISE jacamar

The lesser rhea is named after Darwin (Darwin's rhea).

PAGE 24

Silhouette A is an exact match for the quetzal.

D is the different hawk-headed parrot.

PAGE 25

A + D
B + E
C + K
G + J
I + F
H is the one on its own

M	A	R	M	S	Q	U	I	K	I	L	L
S	N	P	O	A	N	T	E	A	T	E	R
Q	N	O	P	M	R	A	P	G	K	P	O
U	M	R	K	A	O	N	K	E	I	L	I
I	O	C	I	S	R	I	O	E	N	E	G
A	N	U	N	G	G	R	P	C	K	R	U
N	K	P	K	U	I	L	O	E	A	R	S
T	E	I	A	R	M	A	S	T	J	I	L
O	Y	N	R	H	T	H	S	P	O	U	O
S	A	E	R	I	T	T	U	A	U	Q	L
N	L	K	I	N	K	O	M	R	P	S	I
A	A	R	M	A	D	I	L	L	O	T	H
P	A	E	A	T	E	R	K	S	R	E	Y

PAGE 26

PAGE 27

The word POTOO appears 6 times.

PAGE 28

PERU is the country that has the cock of the rock as its national bird.

PAGE 29

- Oropendola
- Scaled antbird
- Blue-faced capuchinbird

PAGE 30

From largest to smallest:

F
D
A
G
C
E
B
H

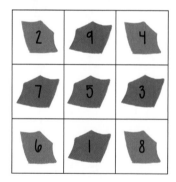

PAGE 31

The full name of this unusual bird is VAMPIRE GROUND FINCH.

PAGE 32

3 foods that albatrosses grab from the ocean: CRABS, SQUID, LOBSTERS

PAGE 33

Macaroni penguins live in Chile, Argentina, the Falkland Islands, and Antarctica.

Magellanic penguins live in Patagonia (the southernmost tip of Chile and Argentina) and the Falkland Islands.

Galápagos penguins live on the Galápagos Islands, west of Ecuador.

Humboldt penguins live in Peru, Argentina, and Chile.

PAGE 34

PAGE 35

There are 20 fish.

PAGE 36

Silhouette C is an exact match for the main picture.

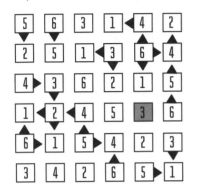

Fact 3 is true: It is the tallest flying bird in South America.

PAGE 37

Pieces A and E are not needed to complete the egg.

The horned screamer lives in these countries: Ecuador, Bolivia, Brazil, Colombia, French Guiana, Guyana, Peru, Suriname, and Venezuela

PAGE 38

17	+	5	=	22
+		+		+
16	+	22	=	38
=		=		=
33	+	27	=	60

A kingfisher has to eat 60% of its body weight each day.

PAGE 39

SHAKESPEARE is the writer they loved so much.

PAGE 40

PAGE 41

	🌰	3	🌰	
	1	4	🌰	
		4	🌰	
🌰	🌰		2	
1				

PAGE 42

The number of each species:

Wood pigeon: 2   Great tit: 3
European robin: 3   Blackbird: 3

PAGE 43

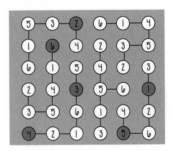

All six facts are true.

UKRAINE has the nightingale as its national bird.

PAGE 44

PAGE 45

These three are missing in the second picture:

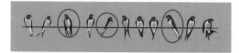

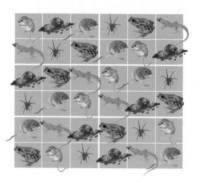

PAGE 46

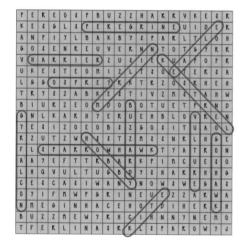

PAGE 47

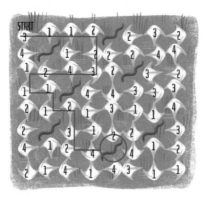

PAGE 48

Silhouette D is an exact match for the golden eagle.

PAGE 50

1. 1 heron is flying
2. A great-crested grebe caught a fish
3. There are 4 female ducks
4. 1 heron and 3 moorhens are on land
5. No ducks are dabbling
6. A moorhen has chicks following it

Puzzle piece B is not needed.

PAGE 51

Lapwings like to eat worms.

The people of northern Europe predict THE START OF SPRING when they see this bird.

PAGE 52

PAGE 53

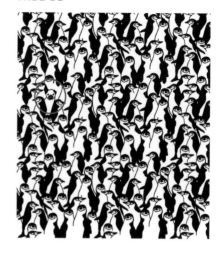

PAGE 54

The answer is B

PAGE 55

There are 2 fewer chicks than adults

PAGE 56

An ostrich could run a marathon in 45 minutes.

PAGE 57

PAGE 58

The shoebill flaps its wings at 150 flaps per minute.

The secretary bird is is the national bird of SUDAN.

PAGE 59

PAGE 60

70% of Africa's dead creatures are cleared away by vultures.

The name Musophagidae means BANANA EATER.

PAGE 61

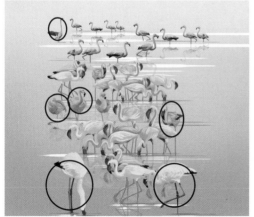

PAGE 62

D is not an exact match.

Other animals egrets follow around: BUFFALO, GIRAFFE, ZEBRA, HIPPOPOTAMUS.

PAGE 63

The meerkats go in this order, with 1 as the oldest:

4 5 1 2 6 3

PAGE 64

Bee A is heading back to the nest.

PAGE 65

A = warthog

B = rhinoceros

C = giraffe

D = zebra

E = hippopotamus

F = buffalo

PAGE 66

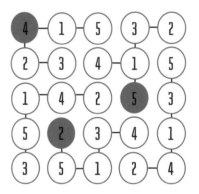

Puzzle piece E is not needed.

PAGE 67

2, 4, and 5 are true.

The mothers have many babies but generally wander off and leave them. Guinea fowl feed during the day time.

An amazing fact about red-billed quelea: There are more of them than any other wild bird in the world.

PAGE 68

Some of the things the red-crowned crane symbolizes: LOVE, LOYALTY, STRENGTH, PEACE, PURITY and LONG LIFE.

PAGE 69

A + D, B + H, C + G, E + I

F is the not part of a pair.

PAGE 70

The ancient Japanese method of fishing is called UKAI.

PAGE 71

The answer is D.

PAGE 72

Here are some words you might have thought of: can, add, dad, acid, kind, rain, rank, dark, card, main, drank, drain, rancid, mankind

PAGE 73

This bird comes next

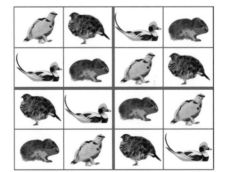

PAGE 74

The male uses MUD AND DUNG to block the hole.

There are 4 spoonbills standing on 1 leg, so there are more standing on 2 legs.

PAGE 75

Eggs B, C, and F are safe.

PAGE 76

—True, they reach 1.5-2 m (5-6.5 ft) tall.

—True

—False, they are dark green.

—False, an emu can have 15 chicks in one brood, sometimes as many as 20.

—True

—True

—False, they can last for weeks without food.

PAGE 77

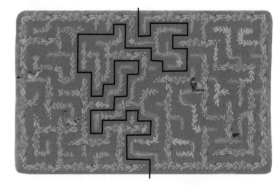

This is the odd one out

PAGE 78

The answer is piece D.

The answer is BUSHMAN'S CLOCK (so called because it usually cackles at dawn and dusk).

PAGE 79

PAGE 80

You might have thought of these words: for, did, odd, pod, fir, rip, drop, fair, soda, road, said, drips, raids, friar, rapid.

But there are lots more!

PAGE 82

1				
	🐰		1	🐰
	🐰	4	4	3
	2	🐰	🐰	🐰
				2

A kiwi egg is 6 times larger than a chicken egg.

PAGE 83

The weebil's claim to fame is it is the SMALLEST BIRD IN AUSTRALIA.

PAGE 84

PAGE 85

Other names for the little penguin:

2. FAIRY PENGUIN   4. BLUE PENGUIN

Number 6 is the wild budgerigar.

PAGE 86

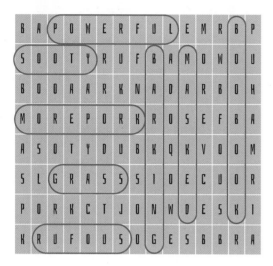

The takahe's main predator is STOAT.

PAGE 87

If the kea turns the bottom wheel
clockwise, the seed will fall into bowl B.

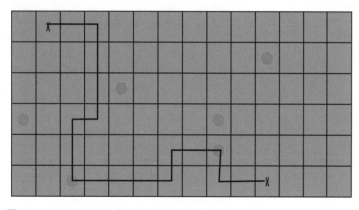

The weka eats two berries along the way.